SLOW PAINTING

HAYWARD GALLERY PUBLISHING

FOREWORD

There is something elemental in the act of painting that distinguishes it from the frantic production of images in contemporary life. Painting is an old, slow art, yet given its enduring presence, we might well ask why, how and through what means painting retains its vitality. Since Hayward Gallery Touring operates on the principle that questions relating to contemporary art should be presented to a wide public across the UK, it seemed the right time to develop our first major painting exhibition in almost 30 years, to consider these ideas and make an argument for a slow approach to painting today.

We invited the writer and art critic Martin Herbert to contribute to this argument and to curate the exhibition. *Slow Painting* focuses primarily on British and UK-based artists whose work spans diverse approaches, from figuration to abstraction and somewhere in between. Most significantly, the exhibition explores multiple ideas of what 'slowness' might mean in relation to recent painting: how it might be present in the making of the work, how the works reward a sustained viewing and how they relate to the continuum of art history. But what the exhibition surveys is less a movement or style than what Martin describes as a 'cultural counter-tendency'. This tendency sustains painting's role as a rewarding repository of time, as a counterbalance to an increasingly accelerating world. It is important precisely because it offers a space of pause and an attentive quality necessary for openness to occur, for both the painter and the viewer.

We are deeply grateful to Martin for his total involvement and commitment to the project, his generous ideas and considered selection of artists, and his illuminating essay. His writing is characterised by an unerring eye and an enduring love for the medium of painting, never losing sight of the bigger picture: what makes art compelling and what it tells us about the times in which we live. It has been a great pleasure to work with him.

Our immense gratitude also goes to all the individuals and institutions who lent works to the exhibition: Arts Council Collection, Daskal Collection, Defares Collection, Collection Nicoletta Fiorucci Russo, Josh Lilley, Lymyfyr Art Consultancy, Paintings in Hospitals, The Pisces Collection, Southampton Art Gallery, Hubert Zandberg and other private collections who prefer to remain anonymous.

When deciding where to present this exhibition we focused on venues and institutions that either already had strong collections of paintings, or were somehow actively involved in the education of the next generation of artists. *Slow Painting* opens at Leeds Art Gallery, and then relocates to The Arts Institution in Plymouth. In Bath, the exhibition spreads across two universities: The Edge, University of Bath, and the Bath School of Art and Design. The exhibition closes in the Highland Museums, also extending across the two sites in Inverness and Thurso, with a distance of over 100 miles between them: visiting both epitomises the essence of slowing down and taking time.

We wholeheartedly thank the following colleagues at these institutions, whose commitment to the project have made it possible: Sarah Brown, Principal Keeper, Leeds Art Gallery; Priscila Buschinelli, Programme and Exhibitions Manager, The Edge, University of Bath; Dr Sarah Chapman, Artistic Director, and Mary Costello, Exhibitions Coordinator, The Arts Insitute, University of Plymouth; Jamie Eastman, Director of Arts, The Edge, University of Bath; Cathy Shankland, Exhibitions Officer, Inverness Museum & Art Gallery; Elizabeth Simpson, Curator of Exhibitions, Leeds Art Gallery; Professor Anita Taylor, Executive Dean, Bath School of Art & Design, Bath Spa University; and Lucy Woodley, Exhibitions Craft & Design, Inverness Museum & Art Gallery.

At the Southbank Centre, we also wish to thank Hayward Gallery Publishing Project Manager Diana Adell for working with consummate professionalism and imagination on this publication with designer Mathias Clottu; as well as Aoife Leach, Hayward General Manager; Alison Maun, Exhibition Bookings and Indemnity Coordinator; Charlotte Pearson, Registrar; James Coney, Senior Technician; and the technical and transport teams.

As always we are grateful for the continuing support of Hayward Gallery Director Ralph Rugoff, and Southbank Centre CEO Elaine Bedell.

Finally, our infinite thanks go to all the artists featured in *Slow Painting*, whose dedication to the art of painting have made this exhibition possible.

Brian Cass, *Senior Curator, Hayward Gallery Touring* Gillian Fox, *Exhibition Organiser*

TAKE YOUR TIME
BY MARTIN HERBERT

Michael Krebber, *Miami City Ballet I*, 2010

In 2009, the critic Raphael Rubinstein published an essay entitled 'Provisional Painting' in *Art in America*, summarising a then-nascent artistic tendency. Bundling together European and American figures such as Raoul De Keyser, Michael Krebber, Mary Heilmann and Christopher Wool, this widely read text anatomised their paintings as deliberately 'casual, dashed-off, tentative, unfinished or self-cancelling'[1], and framed them as part of a continuum of modernist negation. Painting in the early twenty-first century, Rubinstein went on, seemingly could not escape 'a sense of belatedness, a conviction that an earlier generation or artist has left only a few scraps to be cleaned up'.[2] Nonetheless, 'painting must be done, must go on'.[3] A decade ago, this was the right work to spotlight. If one taught in art schools, the influence of provisional painters was visible everywhere: studios full of raw canvases completed after only a few cursory dashes of oil, arranged in groups, loosely suggesting a network. The prime movers did smuggle registers other than refusal into their work – a lyric yearning haunts Krebber's attenuated daubing, for example – but many younger artists did not, and this led to a period of some years when, if you loved painting, you often found it in the arid guise of something overly conceptual, which did not repay lengthy regarding. The art might diffuse anomie and make a paradoxical unity out of continually expressing the sense of an ending, but not much more.

Almost two decades before this, I had gone to art school in Leeds, and trained, initially at least, as a painter. That moment, the early to mid 1990s, was *another* 'endgame painting' one, at least in London. A clutch of British painters, most notably Jason Martin, were essaying a genus of minimal abstraction that drew attention to paint's tactile materiality, denuding it of any other content. Yet this sweeping-up of scraps, as it were, was also part of an even longer timeline of inventive painterly decline stretching back at least to the spirit of Thomas Lawson's 1981 *Artforum* essay 'Last Exit: Painting', which characterised then-leading painters such as David Salle as follows: 'He makes paintings, but they are dead, inert representations of the impossibility of passion in a culture that has institutionalized self-expression.'[4] By the time painting was staggering forward, powered by belatedness, in the early 2000s, it had been getting autopsied for decades. After the early 1980s it only died harder, rising to its feet repeatedly to crash down more loudly and unsubtly.

And yet, by 2019, here was Salle himself, in the *New York Review of Books*, limbering up to write about the German painter Charline von Heyl: 'The art of painting has real vitality at the moment, possibly because the old arguments about whether or not to paint are finally empty husks.'[5] 'Real vitality' is the correct call. Painters may at some point immolate painting again, but of late what has been widely apparent is weariness with being weary. Much painting being made today, both by lodestars such as Von Heyl and by other international artists sitting across different generations, is complexly layered and repays extended eyeing. There is juice left in compositional collision, in getting into trouble on canvas and then vividly getting out of it. A fair bit of contemporary painting reacts to the digital condition – being partly designed up on computers and transferred onto canvas, say – but plenty situates the medium as a locus for an alternative mode of attention to the splintered type engendered by daily scrolling and swiping.

'Slowness', the broad theme connecting the 19 artists in *Slow Painting*, is a cultural counter-tendency that has asserted itself in this century against the acceleration of everyday life, and overarches spheres other than visual art. (For an early shot across the bows, see Carl Honoré's 2004 book *In Praise of Slow*, which in turn references, among other predecessors, Milan Kundera's 1995 novella *Slowness*: 'When things happen too fast, nobody can be certain about anything, about anything at all, not even about himself'[6].) To those who argue that technology is evolving us to move and multitask at its pace, the idea of unhurriedly savouring, say, food, or actual books rather than tweets, or, yes, painting, might seem backward. But painting has always been a realm that allowed for a more protracted unfurling than the rest of life.

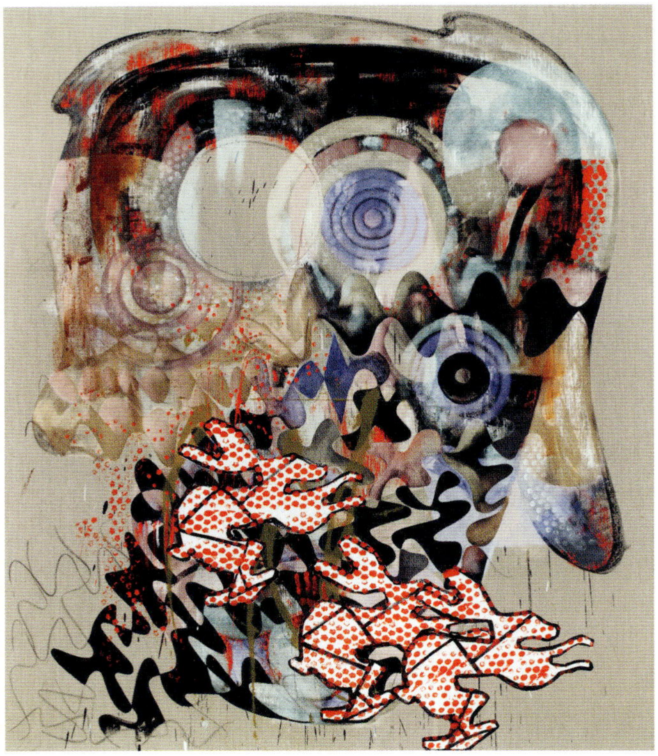

Charline von Heyl, *Manna Hatta*, 2017

In his 2006 book *The Sight of Death: An Experiment in Art Writing*, British art historian T.J. Clark spends six months returning daily to the Getty Research Institute in Los Angeles to look at two Nicolas Poussin landscapes. Clark's diaristic entries record his expansion of understanding vis-à-vis these paintings: how he finds more and different things in them, and how, so he implies, they speak to a fraught, post-9/11 world. By the time he stops, the paintings are not the same ones he first saw, months earlier.

When I first read that book, soon after its publication, my ability to concentrate was not something I worried about. I could see Clark had *more* ability, more patience, but did not feel my own capacities were endangered. I did not own a smartphone then. The iPhone – originally designed as a music player with phone capacities but now a breeding ground for apps engineered to addict the user[7] – was released in 2007, with the slow-burn effects on cognition we are increasingly aware of. Fast forward a decade and more, factor in the rise of social media, and focus has become a battleground. In his 2018 essay collection *ATTENTION: Dispatches from a Land of Distraction*, Joshua Cohen writes: 'Unlike other popular brands of bonkers… *distraction* [emphasis in original] isn't some spontaneous disintegration or unexpected absence of the senses. Instead, it's a gradual disbalancing, which requires only an initial intoxication and then proceeds to intoxicate itself. That's not to say it's a death sentence, however: because, almost uniquely among the mental maladies, *distraction* can be reversed.'[8] Cohen is setting up a succession of texts that depend on close readings of, inter alia, literature, political situations and music, but his argument is applicable elsewhere. Culture, to put it bluntly, might be a halfway house for attention.

Speaking of the artists whose work comprises *Slow Painting* – primarily British and UK-based but part of a larger, informal aegis of the painterly unhurried – it might now be worth unpacking what 'slow' means here. Or rather the various things it signifies, the categories it cuts across beyond hoary divides of figuration and abstraction: slow making, slow revealing, and a patient engagement with the *longue durée* of art history and, in its largest sweep, time itself. Some of these makers bear all the signs of patient, meticulous figuring of the visible on their canvases' surfaces. Their paintings could not be dashed off; they must first have been composed, their parts angled together, then painstakingly realised. Leaving meaning aside at this point, taking in such works is a reminder that painting is a time-based art. Just because nothing is moving, just because you think you can take it all in at once, does not mean you can. (Ask T.J. Clark.)

The eye led close to Gareth Cadwallader's small, pastel-hued, jewel-box canvases might register a figure composition that reverses from comprehensibility to obliquity. In *Milk* (2017, pl. 12), a man is probing a whitish pool of milk on a table, standing by a window that opens onto a crystalline seascape. It is morning, seemingly. But while one is inwardly asking why he is performing this ponderous act, another kind of logic, a compensatory accumulation of formal sense, asserts itself. The gaze, flicking from aspect to aspect, correlates a Hockney-swimming-pool-patterned dressing gown, undulating waters on the other side of the glass, nested clouds, divisions in the apparently snow-dusted landscape that rises above the water. You notice that in this stilled – becalmed – scene, the painting is at once portrait, still life and landscape; and that, somehow, because of the whispery conversation going on between clothing, sea, sky, land, etc., a mysterious unity is being proposed. Moving on to Cadwallader's other paintings, you recognise he is gravitating consistently to moments when people are caught up in analogue fascination – for an egg on a table (pl. 13), a book in a bath (pl. 10); that he is vouchsafing the pleasures of being lost, daydreaming, or hyper-attention to an object; that these paintings are a space where that can happen to you. In his small, self-published 2013 book *Slow Looking: Thirteen Paintings at the National Gallery, London*, David Fraser Jenkins focuses on paintings (by Paolo Uccello, John Constable, Anthony van Dyck, etc.) that foreground the act of looking, that '[show] us by example what it really means to look at the painting, and how the artist expects us to do it'.[9] A parallel process is in play here.

This is just one contemporary artist's repurposing of tight figuration, nevertheless. The intricate rhyming compositions of Benjamin Senior's canvases partly hark back to early modernism, particularly that embedding of the mystical in the everyday practised by Stanley Spencer – whose figures, like Senior's, seem caught up in an unconscious choreography – and Picasso's neoclassicism. His tuned, slightly faded, tertiary-rich colour schemes and vernacular details, though, are contrarily full of slippage – turquoise sunglasses and patterned clothing might either suggest the 1970s, or one of the many 1970s revivals – and the paintings enact themselves in the unspooling present tense of perusal. Seemingly straightforward, if multipart, compositions become increasingly strange, playful, conversant with formalism: blue plastic windmills on a beach divvy the canvas up into chambers and turn it weirdly depthless (*Shade*, 2019, pl. 50); in *Old Town* (2019, pl. 49), as with many of Senior's works, the lower edge doubles as the physical ground on which the sitters – here, appropriately for such ludic art, a couple of men playing chess – sit.

Senior marshals traditionalist skill to renewed ends, overlapping timeframes to wrongfoot the viewer and allow sheer visual pleasure purposefully back into the equation. You look because you want to, and as the painting reveals itself to you it raises questions. In 2008, nine years after finishing her BA, Lucy McKenzie completed a course in *trompe l'oeil* painting at the Van der Kelen Institute for Decorative Art in Brussels. A direct upshot was her *Quodlibet* ('that which pleases' in Latin) paintings. These update a nineteenth-century form of 'conversation piece' work, originally a style of *trompe l'oeil* painting featuring letters, newspaper clippings, playing cards, books, etc. McKenzie's variants mimic bulletin boards, haphazard spreads of images on tables, improvisatory mood boards – images nested within images – and cryptically collapse time while remaining seeded with cues. *Quodlibet XI (Janette Murray)* (2011, pl. 34), for instance, sedulously reproduces ephemera owned by the eponymous knitter, suggesting engagement with manual skills and what might have traditionally been considered women's work. One might expand outward, via the artist's hard-won facture and sustaining of a century-old tradition, to a reconsideration of patient artisanal labour and how one preserves it.

Such works suggest that it might be more forward-thinking to locate new pathways out of the manifold artistic past – untrodden stretches further along roads blocked decades ago, fences leaped – than to find different ways of saying there is no new

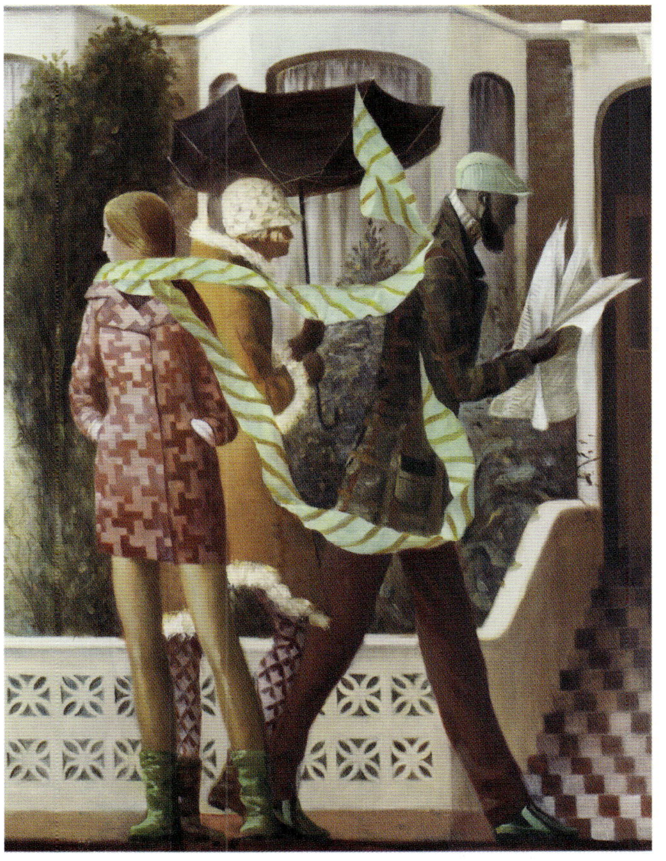

Benjamin Senior, *The Upset*, 2015

ground to break. Modernism in particular went by so fast, a new innovation or a new wrinkle every few months, with barely time for spliced aesthetics to enter the dominant narrative. Artists who did not race forward might be considered minor (even if a figure like British painter Matthew Smith might now fascinate because of his waywardness). In the one-way teleology of the modern, brief strategies were deemed defunct because something new came along, not because the former thing was necessarily out of gas. Postmodernist art, of course, raided the twentieth-century icebox but primarily hitched the spoils together to conceptual ends – saying, approximately, 'no more progress is possible: we, the last ones, can only jumble the timeline'. (The rest, of course, is further history.) But arguably in the 1980s those scrambled parts did not create new affective realities. One might view certain strands of painting in the twenty-first century as released from the anxiety of engaging with modernity's shadow, with progress or otherwise, and rather as reconnecting with something painting did for centuries prior: build thoughtfully on the achievements of predecessors to wrangle ways of expressing what it means to be human, now.

In the case of Paul Housley, these concerns are filtered through the specific plight of the studio-bound painter. That is, wrestling, as some painters will regardless of how fashionable it is, with imposing forebears – with the proximity, in an illustrated art history book, say, of greatness – and wanting to create something emotive and truthful from the struggle. Because this risks self-seriousness, not infrequently Housley positions himself between sombreness and deadpan ridiculousness. His gawky portraits teeter on comedy (*Two Painters,* 2019, pl. 23); his actual wrestlers (*Slow Dance in the Long Game,* 2019, pl. 22), parallels to tortured artistry, are almost overburdened with metaphor. What he creates, resultantly, are compounds that situate painting today as both preposterous and deeply serious. Something of that is conveyed in the fact that while prospecting his lunar, pocked surfaces, you realise you are seeing only the final outcome of a long skirmishing with the motif, or perhaps with all kinds of other motifs buried beneath. This image might not have taken long to make; its slowness is embedded in the fact that it took a long time to find, and there is bathos in this too: all those prior incarnations, and what the artist deemed most worthy was, say, a boggle-eyed face of discontinuous, hectically coloured parts (*Grey Monarch,* 2019, pl. 20).

Paintings such as these constitute, at least in part, an engagement with artistic genres. Now, genre is something outwardly conservative, and as such reverting to it feels outwardly problematic. Note, though, that in the seemingly permissive environs of contemporary art it is hard for anything to create friction. Intelligently tarrying with genre might do so. Mairead O'hEocha's still lives depicted in natural history museums enact distance from the past already: a historical painter might have arrayed birds in their atelier, while she sees them through institutional glass (*Cabinet of Herons, Natural History Museum,* 2018, pl. 36). Her flowers harken back to the memento mori tradition but equally secrete, in their vessels, fragments of portraiture (*Flowers and Herakles,* 2015, pl. 38), not dissimilarly to how Japanese *ukiyo-e* painters would insert a landscape or school of carp into a kimono, a reality within a reality, both existing on the same painted plane. Meanwhile, O'hEocha's colour schemes, which often pull from other artists', offer a melee of temporalities and painted spaces. Her kaleidoscopic pastel tonalities might recall Pierre Bonnard but she paints with a controlled bravura alien to the speckling Frenchman; her flowers and foliage sometimes assume geometric overtones as if nature were turning mathematical, and her subjects can feel blazed with neon light. Most directly, though, here one faces the problem of the revenant: something returned from the past, a parti-coloured ghost. If we have never stopped caring about flowers, landscape, animals, what is the correct language, today, to frame that caring and, conversely, our progressive estrangement from the natural? (The glass of a display case, one might say, is a screen.) The results are self-contradictions, one foot in the past and one in the now, limning a contemporary mindset.

Close in, O'hEocha's brushstrokes combust and her paintings verge on lyric abstraction. In this sense they are figurations *after* abstraction, as are Tim Stoner's Spanish landscapes and floral and arboreal still lives, where the motif is frequently just a pretext (pl. 54–56). Stoner often scrapes back his canvases to reveal the striated layers, archaeological evidence of previous sorties, buried beneath: at once a formal methodology and a pointer towards the multifarious historical layers in the places he paints, these converse unpredictably with the topmost brushwork, snagging the eye as much as the intersections between firm, swooping lines. Here one might think as much of a febrile, skidding Willem de Kooning abstraction as of classical or modern landscape painting; and of space as psychological territory as much as a physical one. The late Carol Rhodes's works (pl. 41–44), with their air of calm control as a means of subterfuge, enact another kind of double vision vis-à-vis the landscape. They are topographical views, for sure, in the artist's signature delicately pallid palette. But they are equally arrangements of line and carved-up space, jittery signs of human habitation in the landscape, factory roofs and industrial estates equalised with a painter's practice of dividing the canvas rectangle into interesting, elliptical segments. The longer you look, the more the picture plane pitches, yaws and switches, seesawing between flatness and depth in a disoriented manner that aligns with the ostensible subject matter.

Doubling is a tool, a delay. You may think you have the art's measure, in that it recalls something, but then – if you follow the cue of the exhibition title and wait, breathe – it veers stealthily to the expansive unknown. Athanasios Argianas's small, salient diptych paintings capsule transformation – they proffer at once modernist-tinged heads, their facture nodding to cubism, and studies of old-fashioned, high-end microphones (pl. 5–6). Argianas, whose practice also incorporates sculpture and canon-based song, is additionally a trained musician, and these paintings suggest a passage between vision and sound, image and language, that is reinforced by their being paired. Something, it is implied, crackles in the gap between repeated takes on the motif. Moving from the first image to the second does not unlock the work but bounces us back to the first; it suggests meaning lies in the emphasised process of change itself and the sustained pinballing subjectivity of reception. Simon Ling's multipart image of skeletons, or *a* skeleton repeated, is explicitly concerned with the act of looking (*Untitled*, 2018, pl. 33). As with many of his works, the subject is backlit with the orange glow of neon underpainting that suggests an animist vitalism in an immobile, literally dead, subject; typically for Ling, too, the composition bounces the eye around, an image that at first glance appears comprehensible becoming more complex and less orderly as you continue parsing: like a familiar word looked at too long, it descends towards the non-concrete. A depicted *thing* becomes an entrée to an excursus on the inner lives of objects, and on the positive stress – eustress – of pausing and peering, dealing with the convolutions of the visible.

If the styles of slowness tabulated above mostly involve slow making, slow seeing and a reconsideration and refreshing of art-historical modes, other artists use painting as an aperture onto extensive cultural histories. Michael Simpson's paintings – while encoding temporality through such devices as wandering shadows on his diptychs and triptychs, and indirectly through fresco-like textures designed to snag the eye and signal the past – have long engaged in iconographic terms with what he has consistently called the 'infamous' history of organised religion, primarily Christianity. He works, painstakingly, by modulating motifs such as the confessional and the 'leper squints' cut into the side of ancient churches, which in his work suggest not only the exclusion of the infirm but, in a secular world, being locked out of hopes for something better. Simpson is not a literalist, however; and some of his paintings, such as *Squint 59* (2017, pl. 53), with its carceral cage and multiple 'squints', point to his concerns while radiating an air of ambient anxiety. The image, a condensation of captivity read through modernist gridwork, suggests, in the context of the artist's oeuvre, the punishment of heretics in one era and the rationalist aesthetics of a world without God, but it does not quite *illustrate* anything. It is a container for apprehensive thought.

Simpson's paintings need temporal legroom to open up, for their white backgrounds to reveal themselves not as negative space but embodied atmospheres, pregnant with invisible occurrences. Lubaina Himid's 2016 series of paintings *Le Rodeur* equally stashes a sour chronicle behind a deeply composed frontage. These paintings refer to atrocities against African slaves on colonisers' ships, here specifically the French vessel for which the sequence is named, which in 1819 was overloaded with enslaved Nigerians and entered a hellscape of contagious blindness, panic, suicides and murders. But Himid, resistant to showing slaves as victims, elects to present ambiguous, stilled, hieratic scenes featuring black figures in fine contemporary dress, with the roiling waves outside a window, that meet the written history at an oblique, ironical angle (*Le Rodeur: The Exchange*, 2016, pl. 19). Michael Armitage, too, seeks a painterly truthiness beyond depiction of events (pl. 7–9). His dreamily coloured and lithely drafted works, painted on lubugo, a traditional bark cloth from Uganda, speak to his East African – specifically, Kenyan – heritage. Yet while Armitage's paintings relate to specificities, from terrorist attacks to a plane crash he witnessed as a teenager, to public gatherings during electioneering, they mingle them with imagery pulled from a diversity of other, unrelated sources and pivot frequently into liquefied near-abstraction – such that

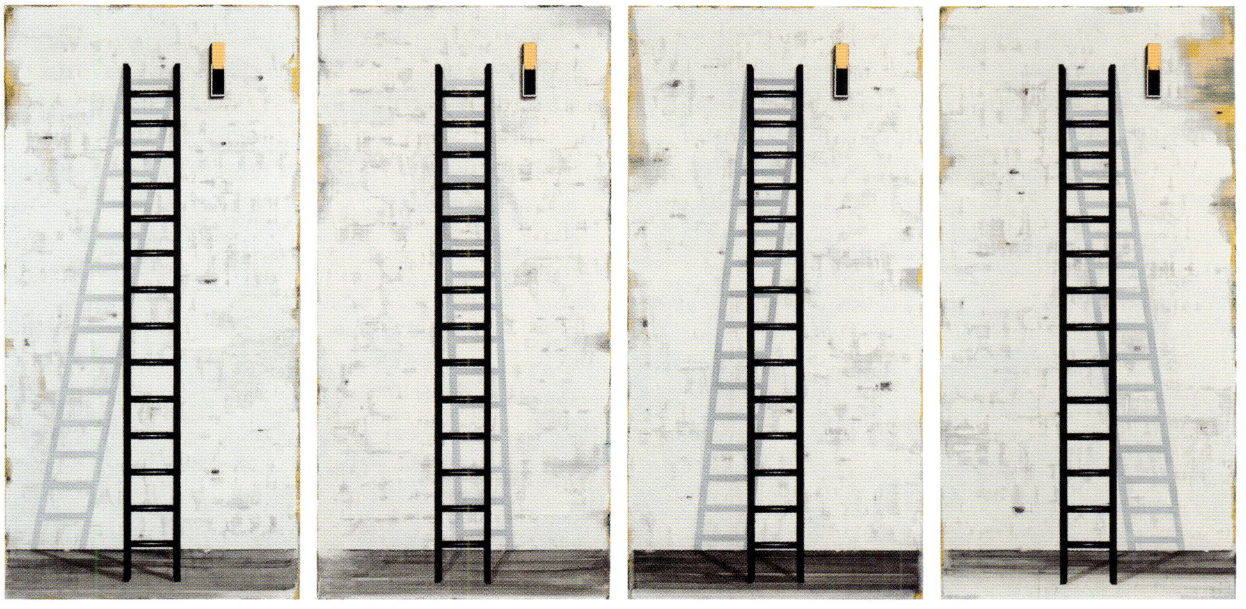

Michael Simpson, *Squint 44*, 2017

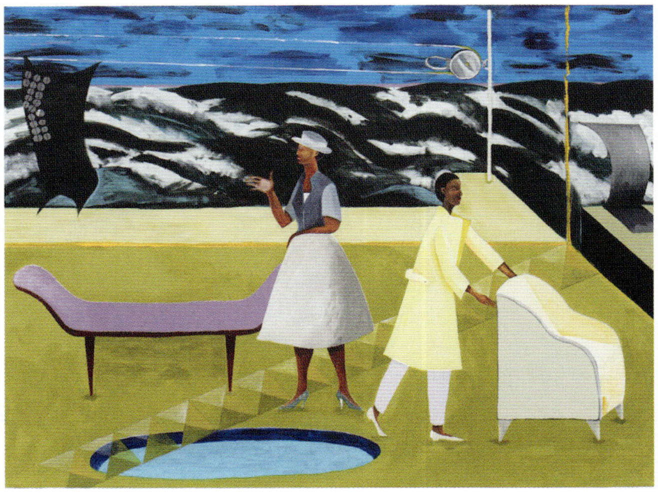

Lubaina Himid, *Le Rodeur: The Pulley*, 2017

the images become depictions not of events but of a racing mind working to process them, seemingly without resolution, perhaps turning in circles.

Just as a poem can be extremely short, just a few precisely chosen words, but still create friction, irresolution or vast and shifting mental images, the reception time of a painting has little to do with how much visual information it contains (or, again, how long it took to paint). Allison Katz's paintings operate in a purposeful conundrum style. Their parts are recognisable, sociably readable: body parts, often, from mouths to limbs to breasts, with suggestions – such as the punning phrase 'All Is On' used as ersatz eyes and mouth to create a sketchy portrait (*AKgraph (All Is On)*, 2016, pl. 29) – that they are those of the maker herself. Still, Katz frequently juxtaposes these with a found or generic image – an antique illustration involving elves (*Elf-Esteem*, 2017, pl. 30), a snow-swept balcony (*Snowglobe*, 2018, pl. 28) – or shrouds another image under the main one (*Double Hunger*, 2015, pl. 31). We are invited to guess at a personal connection between the artist and her visual materials, and to think we can know something about her as a result; but this, taken in tandem with Katz's shape-shifting approach to aesthetics, might all be a deceit, the whole an inquiry into the possibility of expressing selfhood through painting. What you see is built on epistemological quicksand, as the viewer *feels* to be accumulating more information about the elusive maker – is that scar really hers? – but a pathway to certainty is denied.

Caragh Thuring's works are painted on canvases woven, in collaboration with weavers from Belgium and Suffolk, from images of her own previous paintings: a nudge to the fact that meaning-making here might operate not on the level of the individual, self-contained image but between works, and with the requirement of some backstory. On the one hand, she paints specific industrial elements over her tartans (*Down Bubble*, 2017, pl. 58) – tartan itself being allusive, its colours historically used to differentiate clans; the combination suggesting a narrative. Yet rogue elements pop up in the mix: a mischievously sexualised cactus (*Roger*, 2018, pl. 57), an erupting volcano (*Double Kiss*, 2018, pl. 59), point to Thuring's long-standing interest in these forces of nature. As such, crowbarred open by disconnections and stutters, these are reflexive paintings about the contingency of meaning, the act of reading a painting and how that might be pleasurably stymied ('You don't want to arrive anywhere – there is no destination,' the artist has said[10]), how a viewer might gain information and structure but, again, not necessarily illumination.

Some of Sherman Mern Tat Sam's paintings (pl. 45–48) take up to ten years to complete: in this regard, he is not far from Paul Housley or, on occasion, Tim Stoner, but Sam is an abstractionist through and through. Often composed on lightly misshapen little pieces of board, his art is one of steady accommodation to inevitable imperfection. The parts jostle together to find a comfortable shared position, and this position itself seems temporary: there is a sense that some constituents of the image are sliding into view from a former life outside the frame. Life gets trapped in the wonky contours. That the paintings have a past (and maybe a future) is reconfirmed when you move in close and see ghostly glazes, penumbra; much, you suspect, has been scraped off, but enough of the decision-making process remains, and equally apparent is the extent to which Sam's compressed range of colours sing to each other.

Sam purveys a style of abstraction that snags the eye and whose seeming offhandness is deceptive, a kind of wrought casualness. Varda Caivano operates in a somewhat related register: her paint, often thinned and loosely brushed, creates colloquies between overlapping regions and her diaphanous compositions can appear in dialogue with multiple past eras, from abstract expressionism and its passage into lyrical abstraction and colour fields, as well as early modernist landscape painting (pl. 14–17). But Caivano's paintings each have an uncanny self-containment even while they accept organisation into sympathetic groups. They are febrile problem-spaces, evoking things and then stepping lightly away. You can look at them lengthily without plumbing their depths; they also evade reduction in linguistic terms.

This leads to another, crucial aspect of paintings built for sustained attention. While much art and even some painting now appears designed to 'pop' on social media, these canvases require a physical presence inhabiting the enlivened air in front of them. It might once have been a given that there is

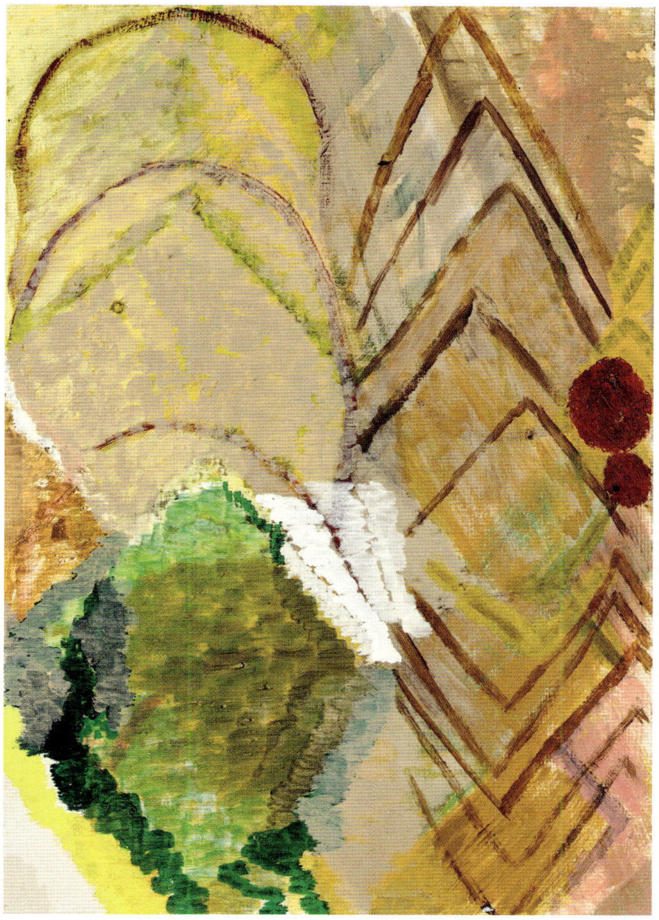

Sherman Mern Tat Sam, *Stuck on Repeat*, 2011

a difference between a physical artwork and its reproduction: the ubiquity of digital imagery, though, now means that the case has to be stated again. Paintings like Caivano's, with their rich blues and pinks and smoky purples and grainy, subtle textures, exhale atmospheres that cameras cannot quite catch. A great painting in the flesh will, improbably, make it hard to wrest your gaze away; a photograph on a screen will not; the physics behind this are unclear. This is particularly true of Yelena Popova's work, which, in some cases, sits at the very edge of visibility (pl. 39–40). Popova is deeply engaged with the idealism and darkness of the modern era; radiation, its lingering presence in the earth in Russia, is one engine of her art, geometric abstraction is another and spectral odalisques are a third. Her art, in its deep evanescence, can appear to be gently manifesting – again like an unreconciled ghost – or fading away, and is chancily activated by changing light and the motility of the viewer, who here serves as a co-composer.

When painting that takes time to evaluate speaks of a longer timeline, the viewer becomes aware of this duality: the duration of observation nestling within a stretch of the medium's own history. With their glowing ellipses in darkness, Darren Almond's *Somewhere Between* series (2018, pl. 1–4), painted in aquacryl on aluminium, at first blush suggest mystically inclined abstractions that might have been made in the 1920s. In actuality these are speculative renderings of a scientific-philosophical principle in atomistic theory, the *clinamen* or 'swerve', formulated by the first-century Roman poet Lucretius in his book *On the Nature of Things* (c.50 BC), which argues that for matter to exist, atoms in a vacuum must have swerved together; one might correlate Lucretius' insight with the more recent discovery of gravitational waves, a kind of swirling ripple effect in the universe based on the inconstancy of gravity, and we may have the origins of everything. Almond's art thus tracks back first twenty centuries and then to the beginning of time. It is, in this regard, the largest scale upon which *Slow Painting* enacts itself, and within which all its other histories are couched.

If this project began with one artist, it is Merlin James, whose fluent swerving between, and collapsing together of, painterly modes – figurative and abstract, sexualisation and abstraction, tender studies of landscape and formalist attention to the backs of his canvases, all somehow unified by a virtuosic, rough-edged touch (pl. 24–27) – makes him something of a lodestar here. I am resistant to stepping too heavily on James's art with explicatory sentences. Perhaps suffice to say that the selection of works here represents a constellation, bouncing inference back and forth, yet each painting is a miniature world of its own; and that he is a painter who has assumed the freedom of postmodernism to paint in any manner he likes, without his work ever feeling illustratively theoretical; it presents, rather, as consistently personal and emotive. It was James who gave me the *Slow Looking* book mentioned above, and it is not surprising he had it. What his art represents, in one sense, is the preservation, without any archaism, of a committed, intuitive yet intellectual approach to painting, the perpetuation of a language of great delicacy and subtlety: a language preyed upon by, it seems, expanding visual illiteracy.

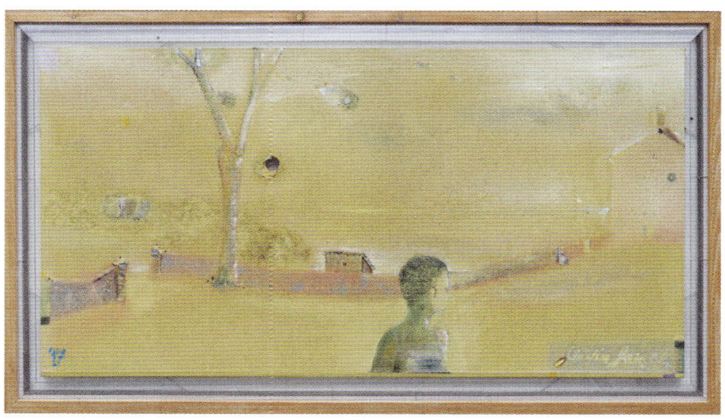

Merlin James, *The Vale*, 2017

Images are everywhere in our culture, particularly our digital culture, but we glimpse most of them for seconds, partly because they are *designed* to be seen for seconds. Slowness, as addressed by this convening of artists, is a testing of what happens if you stay with something. (John Cage, who understood this principle of forbearance well, famously offered the Zen-inflected advice that if one finds something boring after two minutes, try it for four, and so on; eventually it will not be boring.) The ability to see painting, to see what has been put there by someone of great talent, is not innate. It grows, and it grows only in looking. When the aforementioned David Salle analyses the bold stylistic patchworking of Charline von Heyl's work, or when others explore what is going on in the densely plotted work of artists such as Njideka Akunyili Crosby, Nicole Eisenman, Jana Euler, Kerry James Marshall, Laura Owens and Dana Schutz – to name a handful of artists whose works fall outside the confines of this exhibition but who go to bat these days for painterly intelligence – it is the product of a long apprenticeship of not only making but also directed gazing. That teaches one patience, gives one a comparative repertoire: an accumulation of memories of when, for instance, you looked not only at contemporary and modern painting but at a Vermeer or a Rembrandt or a Titian. What first drew you to the painting was gradually overtaken by a small avalanche of other aspects, the sly compositional rhymes that gave the painting its immediate impression of rightness, the for-the-time risks, the bravura details.

These artists do not constitute a movement, or even anything as organised as a tendency. At most, they are a broad counter-tendency to one in which everything is packaged for ever-quicker consumption, shorter attention spans – a counter-tendency that stretches back to labours of love such as Jay DeFeo's legendary *The Rose,* begun in 1959 and finished, when the paint-encrusted, multi-layered work weighed almost a ton, in 1966.[11] In his 1986 novel *An Artist of the Floating World*, Kazuo Ishiguro writes of a painting class that divides its students into two styles: the productive, pacey 'Engineers' and the 'Backwarders', the latter so called because they keep pausing to step back from their canvases and assess them, and operate glacially as a result. Mapping this binary onto the recent history of painting, it is not the case that the artists considered here emerged *after* the 'provisional' artistry mentioned at this essay's outset; art history, we are now aware, does not simply move in phases. Rather, during the rises and falls of various 'endgame' painting movements stretching back to at least the 1980s – when Michael Simpson and Merlin James, in particular, were already working – other artists have dug in, remaining steadfast to painting as a locus of rich complication only accessible to those who either create slowly or work towards pictorial invention that requests persistent beholding, and that scatters gifts to the patient observer. *Slow Painting* is a window onto this world.

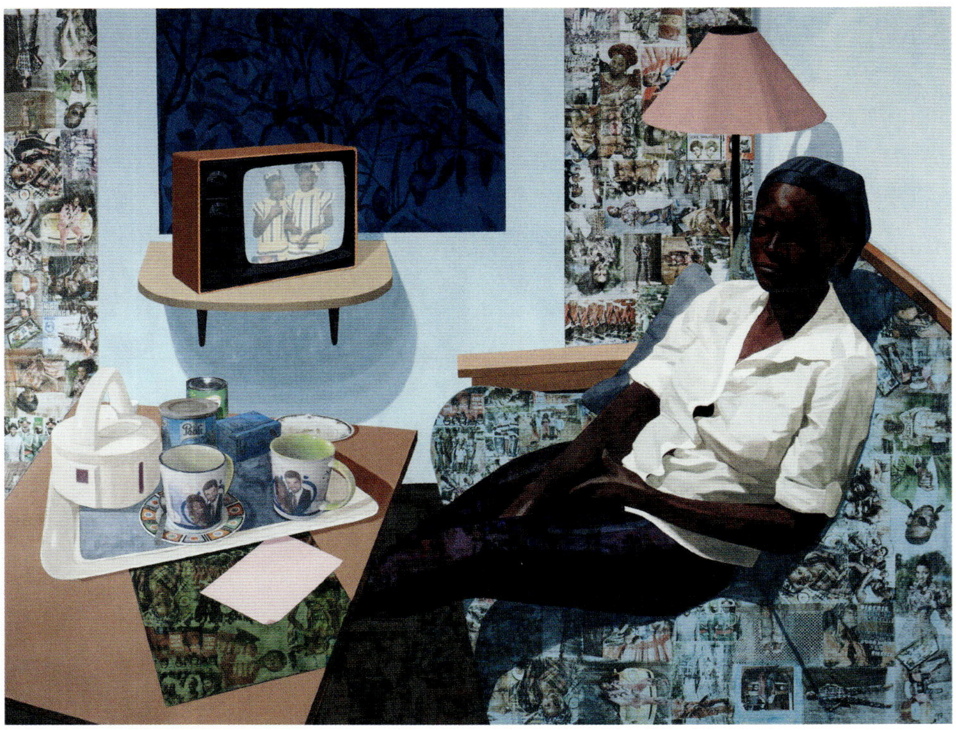

Njideka Akunyili Crosby, *Super Blue Omo*, 2016

1 Raphael Rubinstein, 'Provisional Painting', *Art in America*, May 2009 [artinamericamagazine.com/news-features/magazines/provisional-painting-raphael-rubinstein/, accessed 10 June 2019]
2 Ibid.
3 Ibid.
4 Thomas Lawson, 'Last Exit: Painting', *Artforum*, October 1981, p. 42
5 David Salle, 'Houdini with a Brush', *New York Review of Books*, 9–22 May 2019, p. 16
6 Carl Honoré, *In Praise of Slow* (London: Orion Books, 2004), p. 6
7 For more on this subject, see Adam Alter, *Irresistible* (New York: Penguin Press, 2018) and Cal Newport, *Digital Minimalism: On Living Better with Less Technology* (London: Portfolio Penguin, 2019)
8 Joshua Cohen, *ATTENTION: Dispatches from a Land of Distraction* (London: Fitzcarraldo Editions, 2018), p. 6
9 David Fraser Jenkins, *Slow Looking: Thirteen Paintings at the National Gallery* (self-published, 2013), p. 5
10 Artist in conversation with Glenn Brown, *Caragh Thuring: Volcano*, exh. cat. (London/Naples: Thomas Dane Gallery, 2019), unpaginated
11 I also claim no great originality for this concept, and indeed discovered, after conceptualising this exhibition and choosing the artists, that the aforementioned *Art in America* published an article entitled 'Slow Painting' in February 2018, with an entirely different (and entirely American) group of artists mentioned, and which built on *another* recent article about slowness in painting, John Yau's 'The Pleasures of Slow Paintings', *Hyperallergic*, 24 September 2017 [hyperallergic.com/401798/suzan-frecon-recent-oil-paintings-david-zwirner-2017/, accessed 25 June 2019]. One could go back, if desired, at least as far as Honoré de Balzac's famous story *The Unknown Masterpiece*, 1831. See Honoré de Balzac, *The Unknown Masterpiece* (New York: New York Review Books, 2001), pp. 3–44

PLATES

DARREN ALMOND

1. Darren Almond, *Somewhere Between I*, 2018

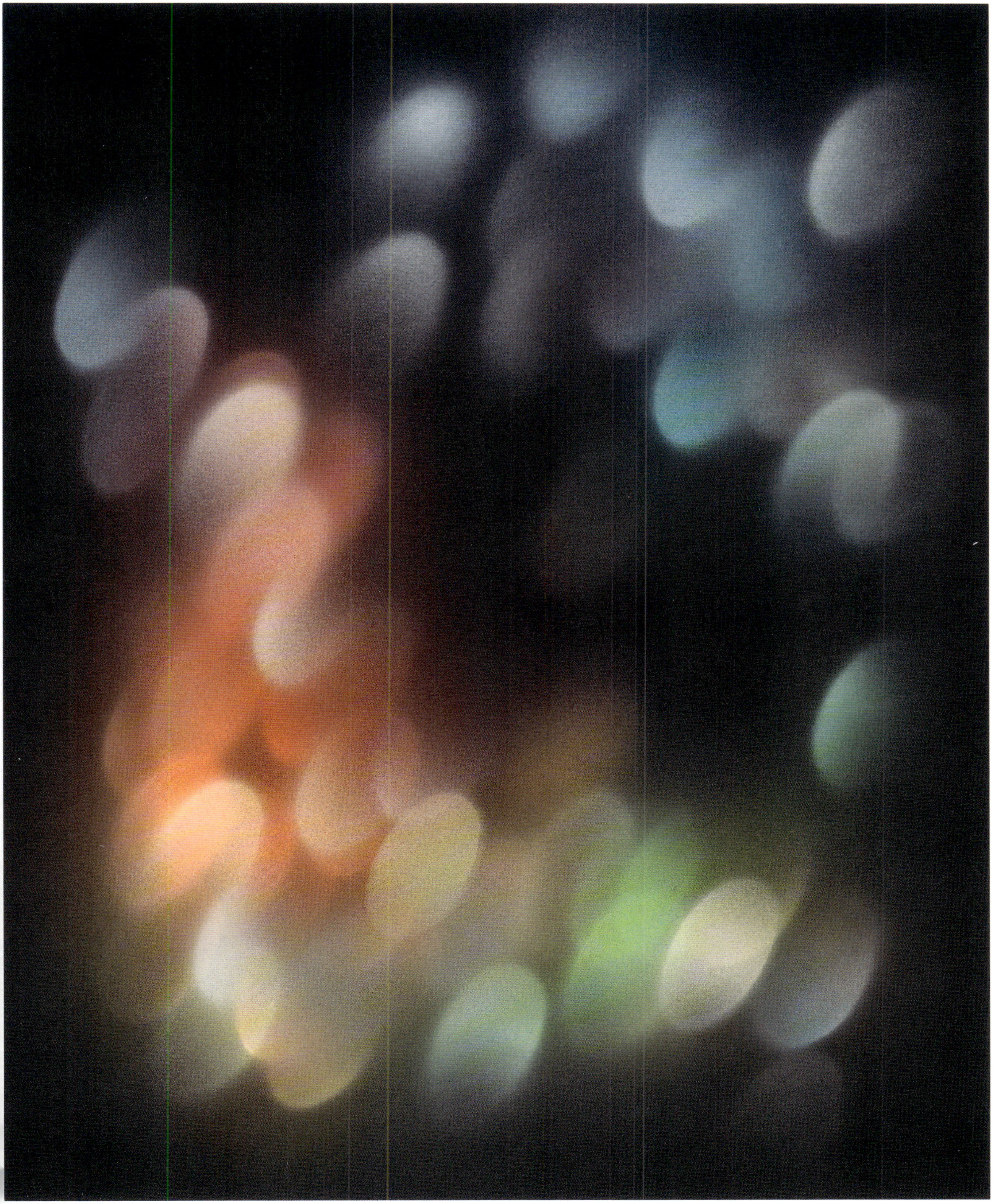

2. Darren Almond, *Somewhere Between VII*, 2018

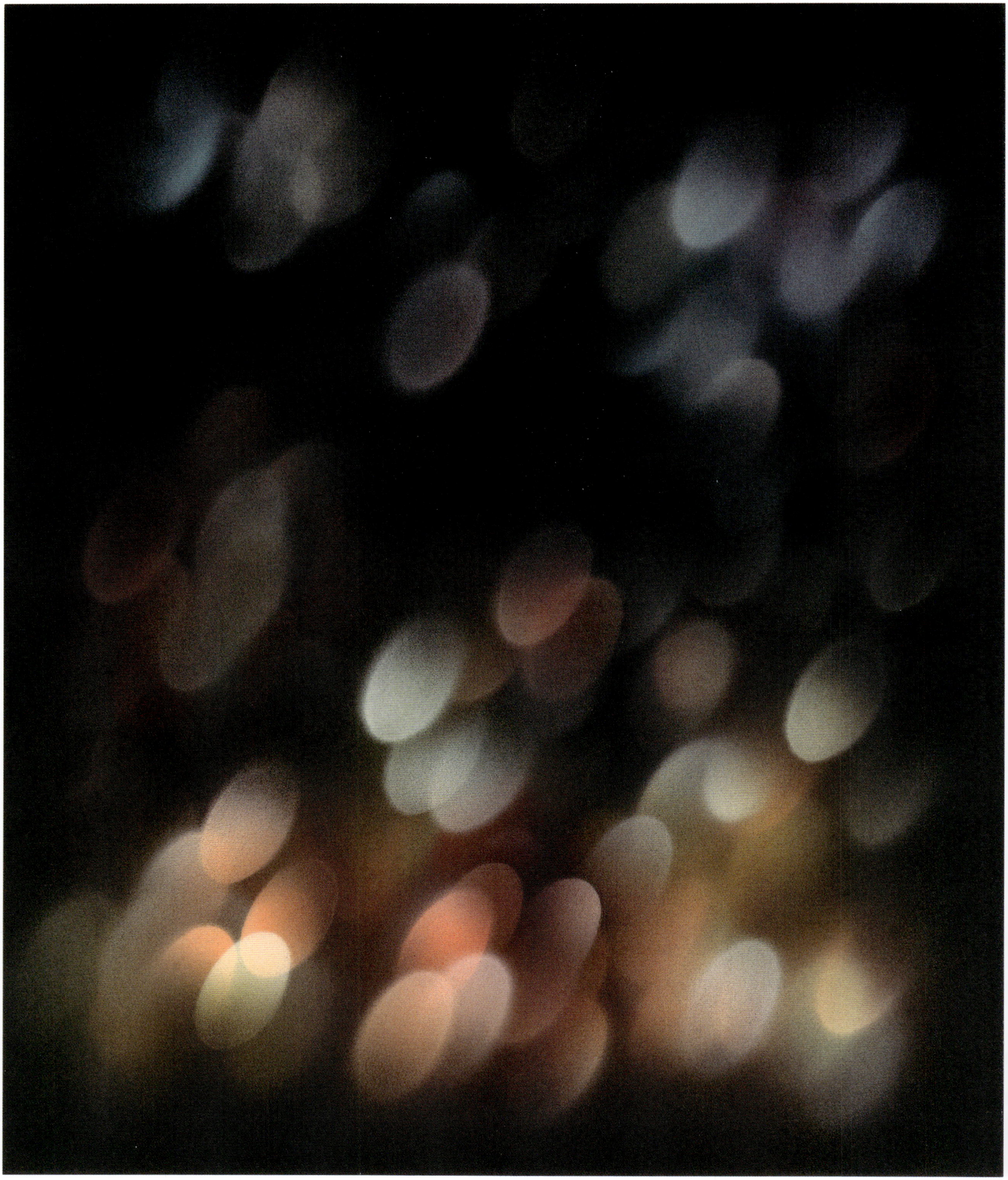

3. Darren Almond, *Somewhere Between XVI*, 2018

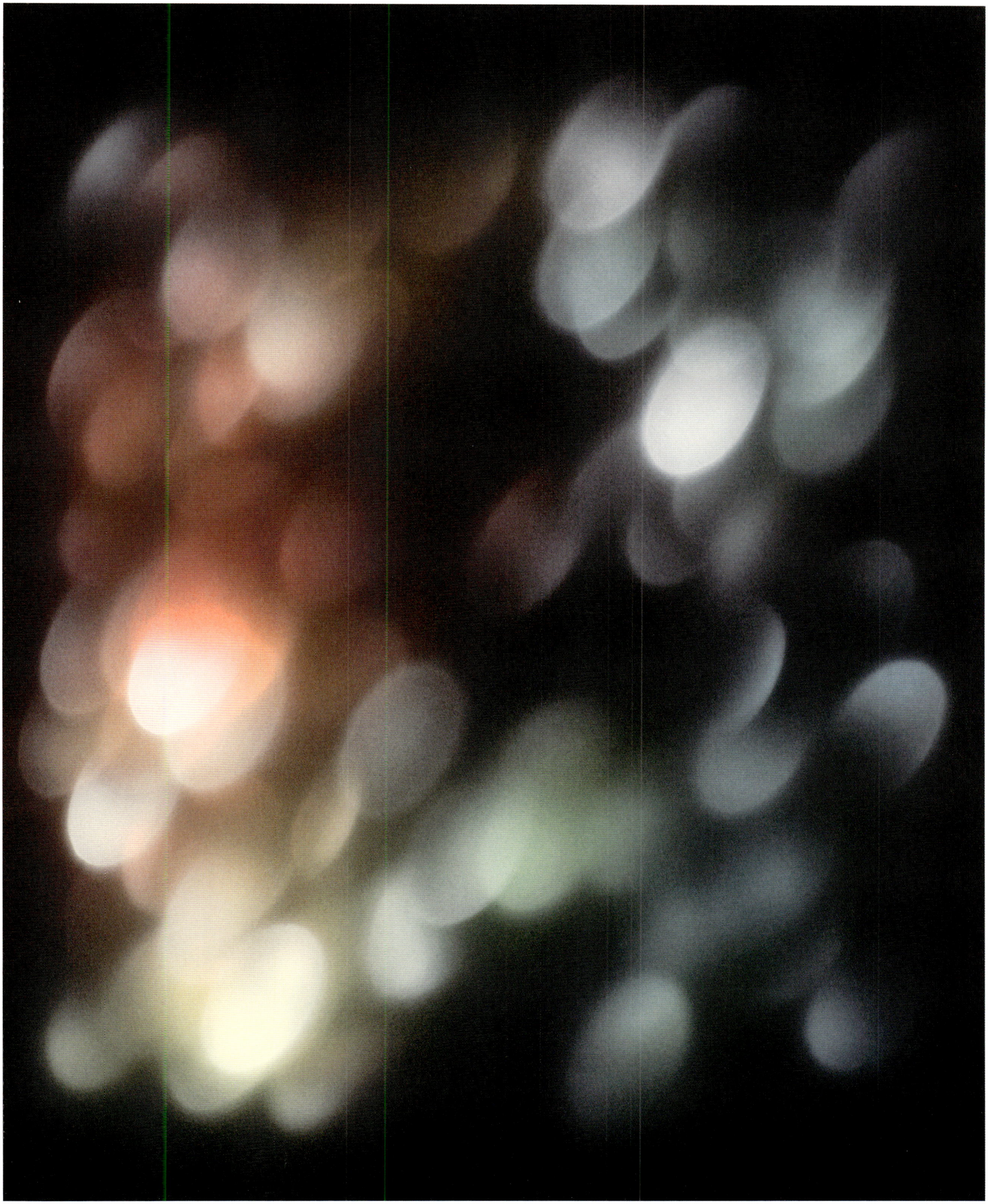

4. Darren Almond, *Somewhere Between XVIII*, 2018

ATHANASIOS ARGIANAS

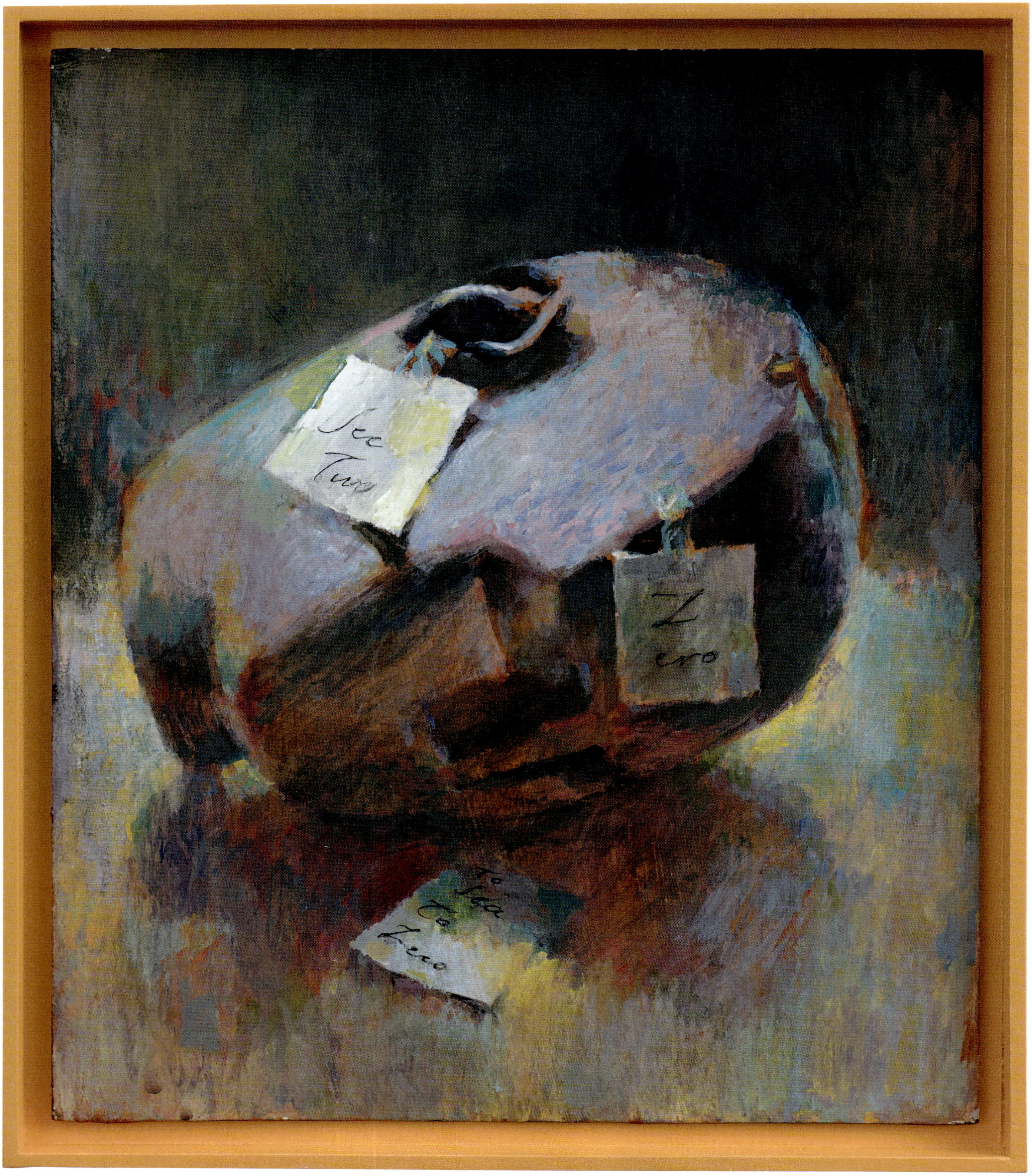

5. Athanasios Argianas, *reading paintings (no1, binaural microphone & post-it notes)*, 2019

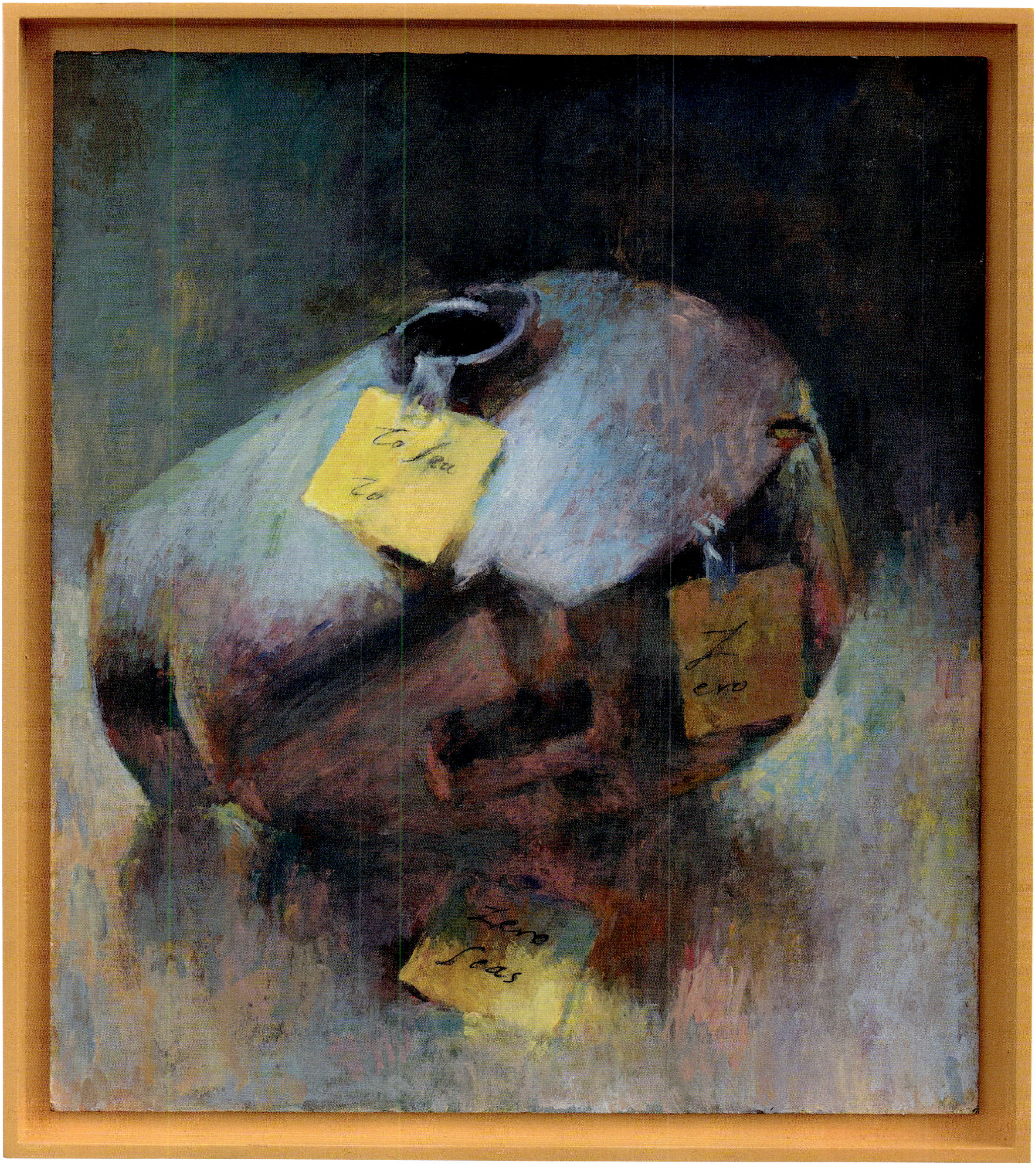
Zero
Zero Seas

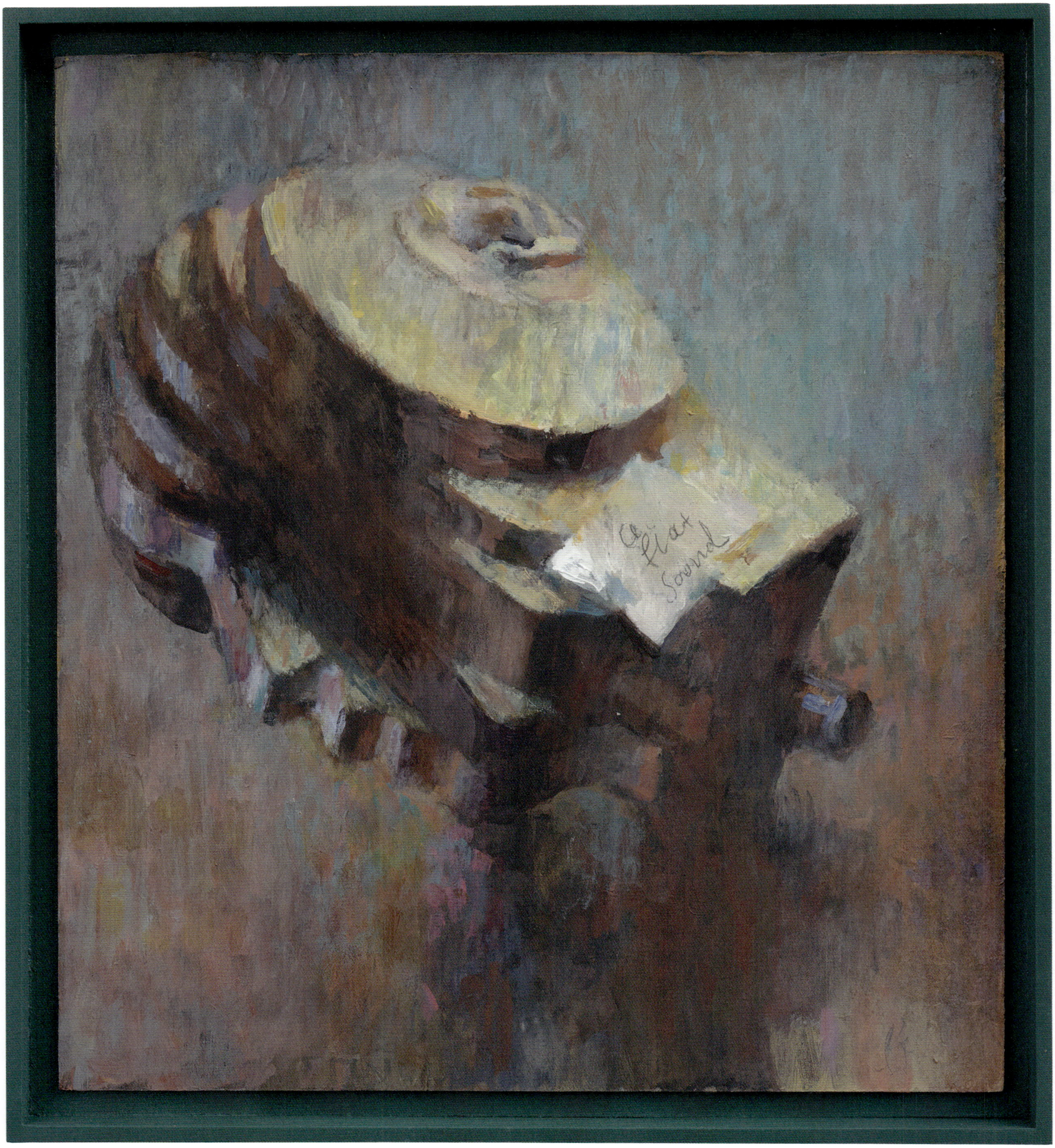

6. Athanasios Argianas, *reading paintings (no2, binaural microphone & post-it notes)*, 2019

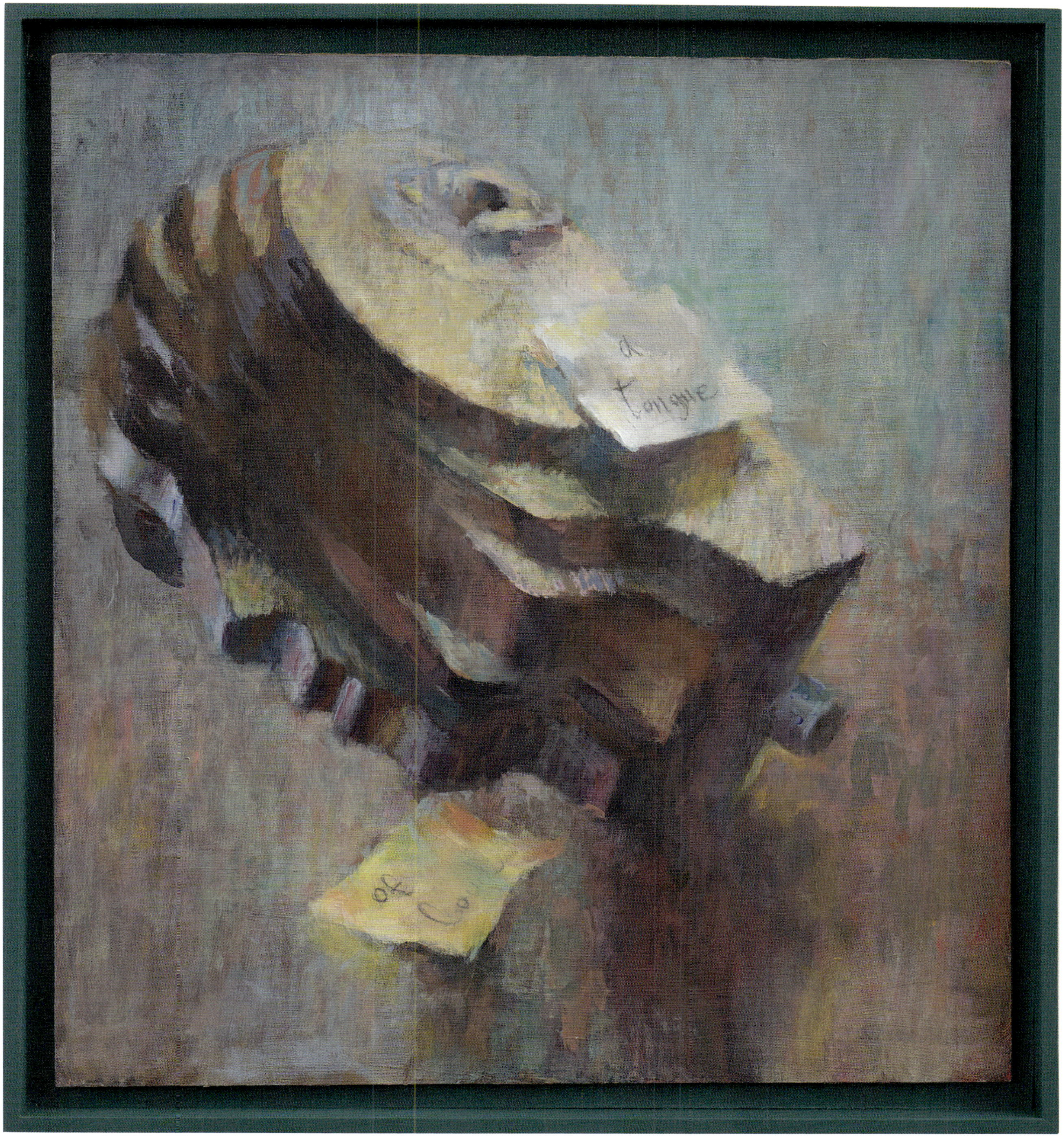
a
tongue
of

MICHAEL ARMITAGE

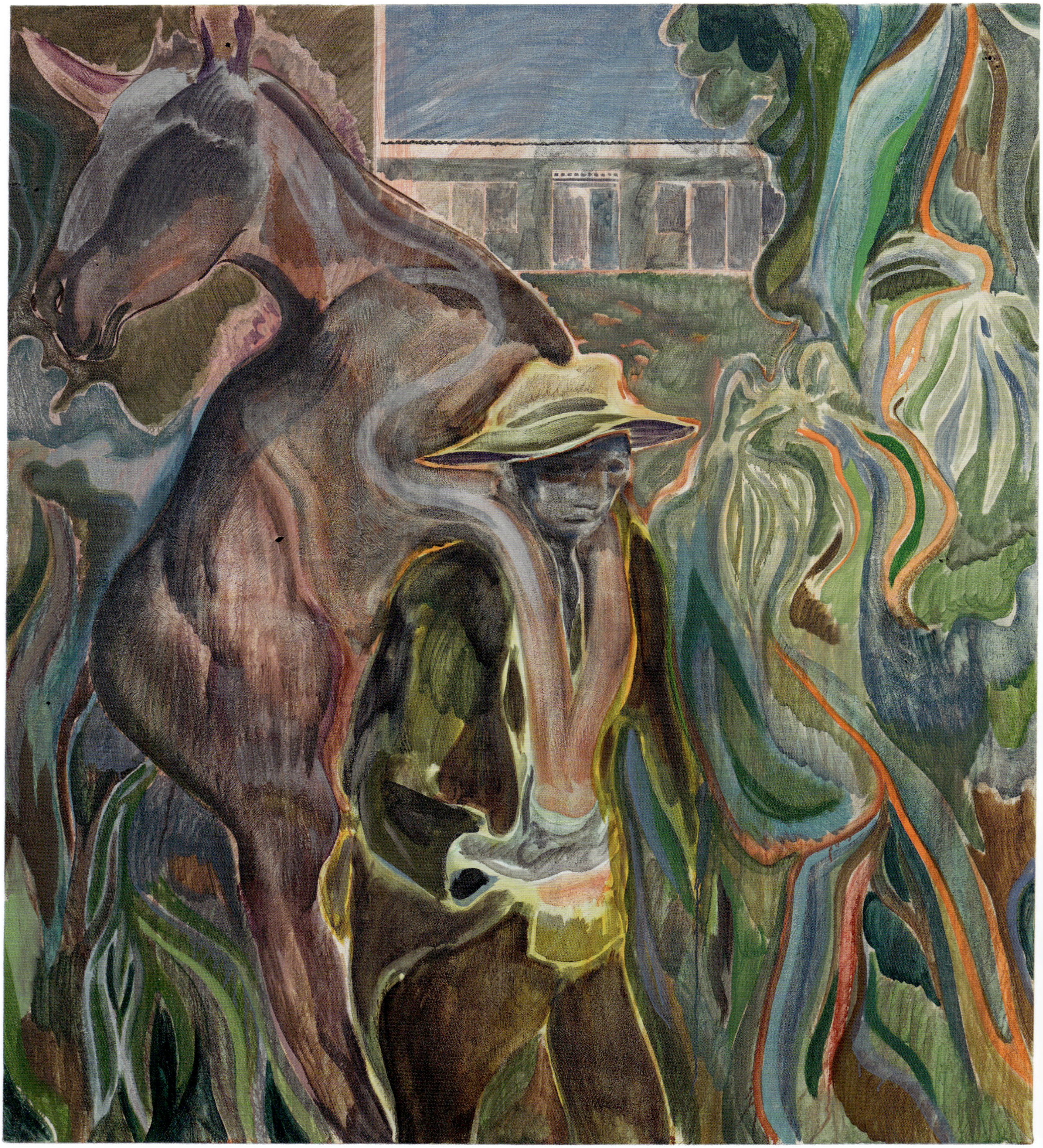

7. Michael Armitage, *Kariakor*, 2015

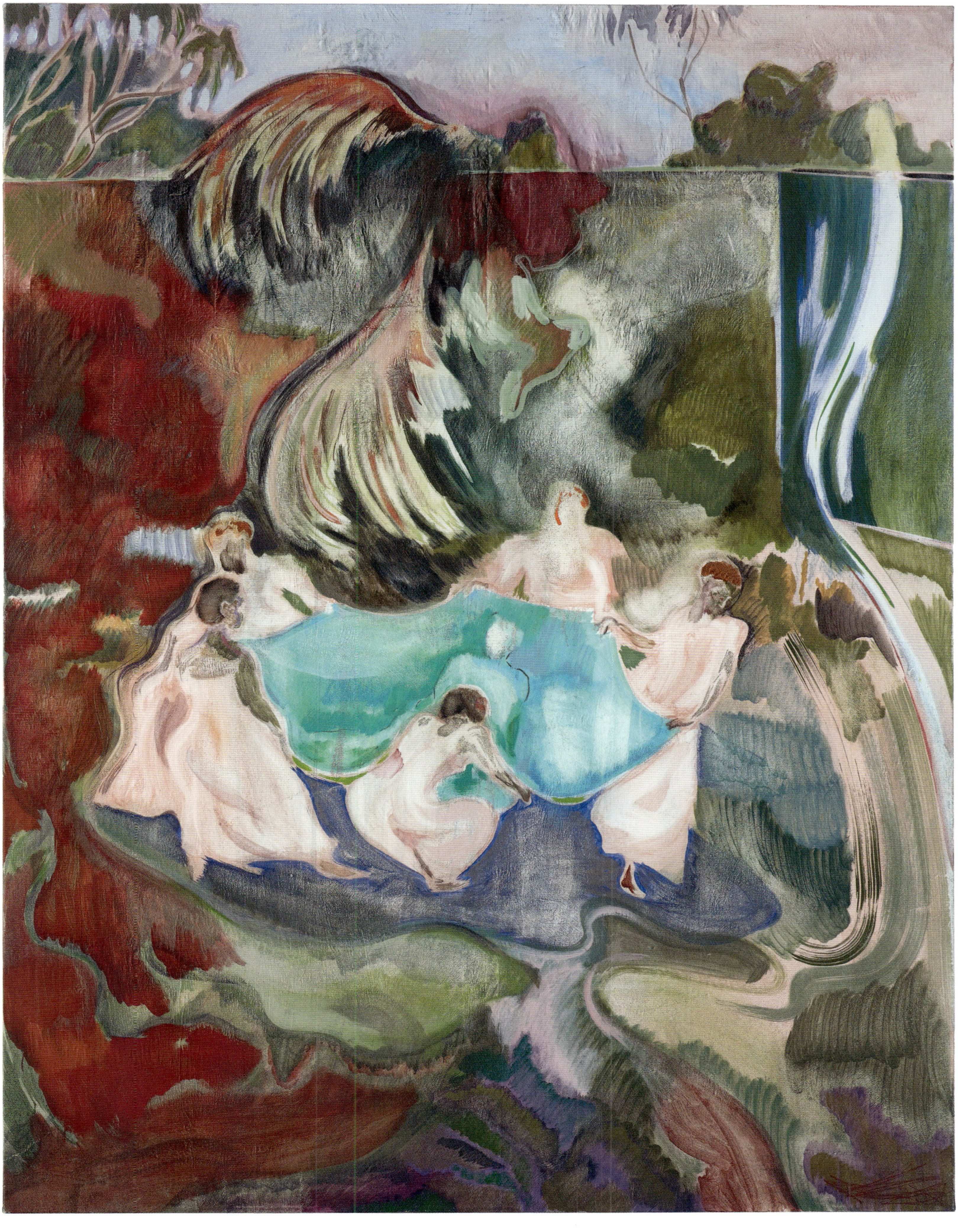

8. Michael Armitage, *Mpeketoni*, 2015

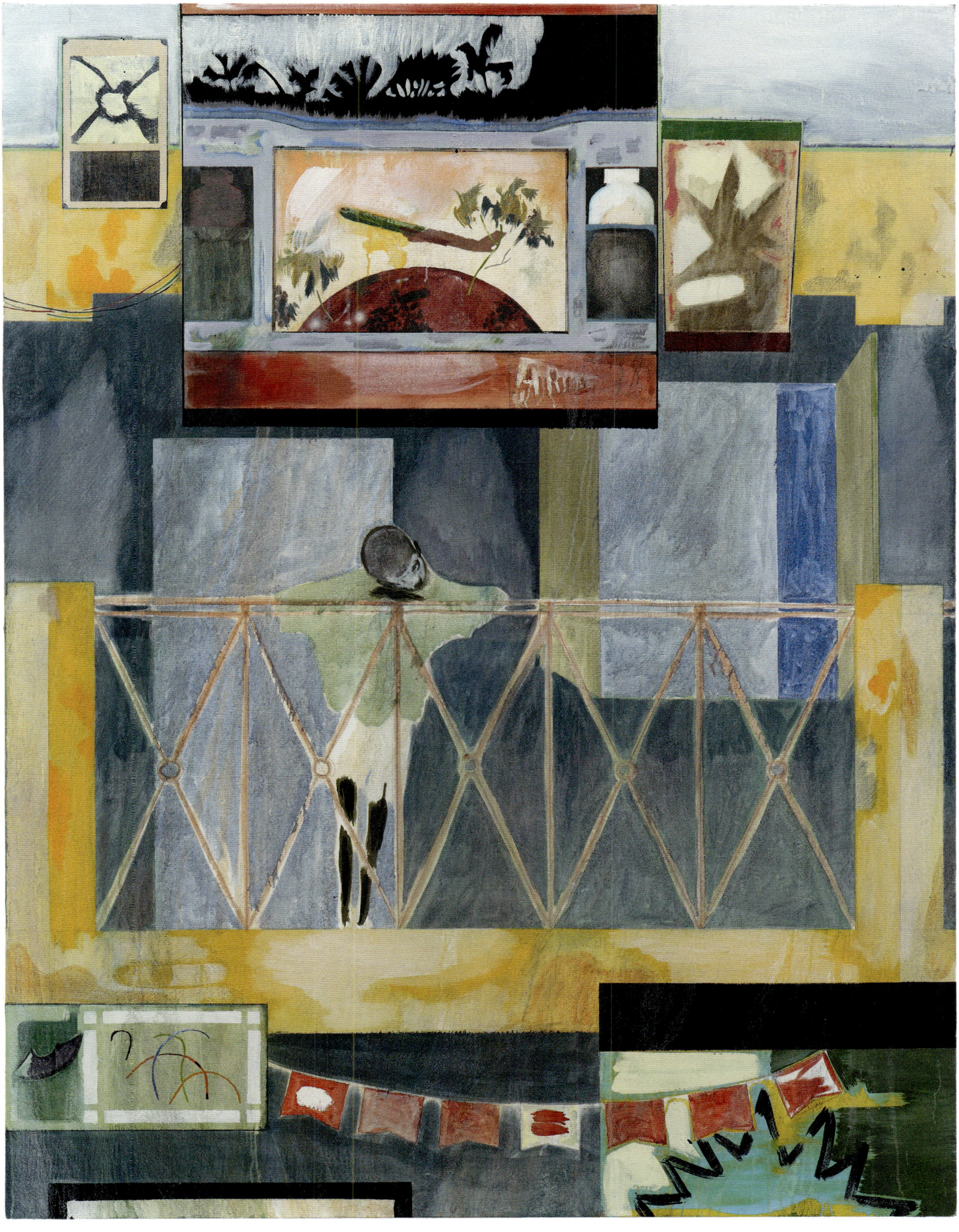

9. Michael Armitage, *Balcony*, 2013

GARETH CADWALLADER

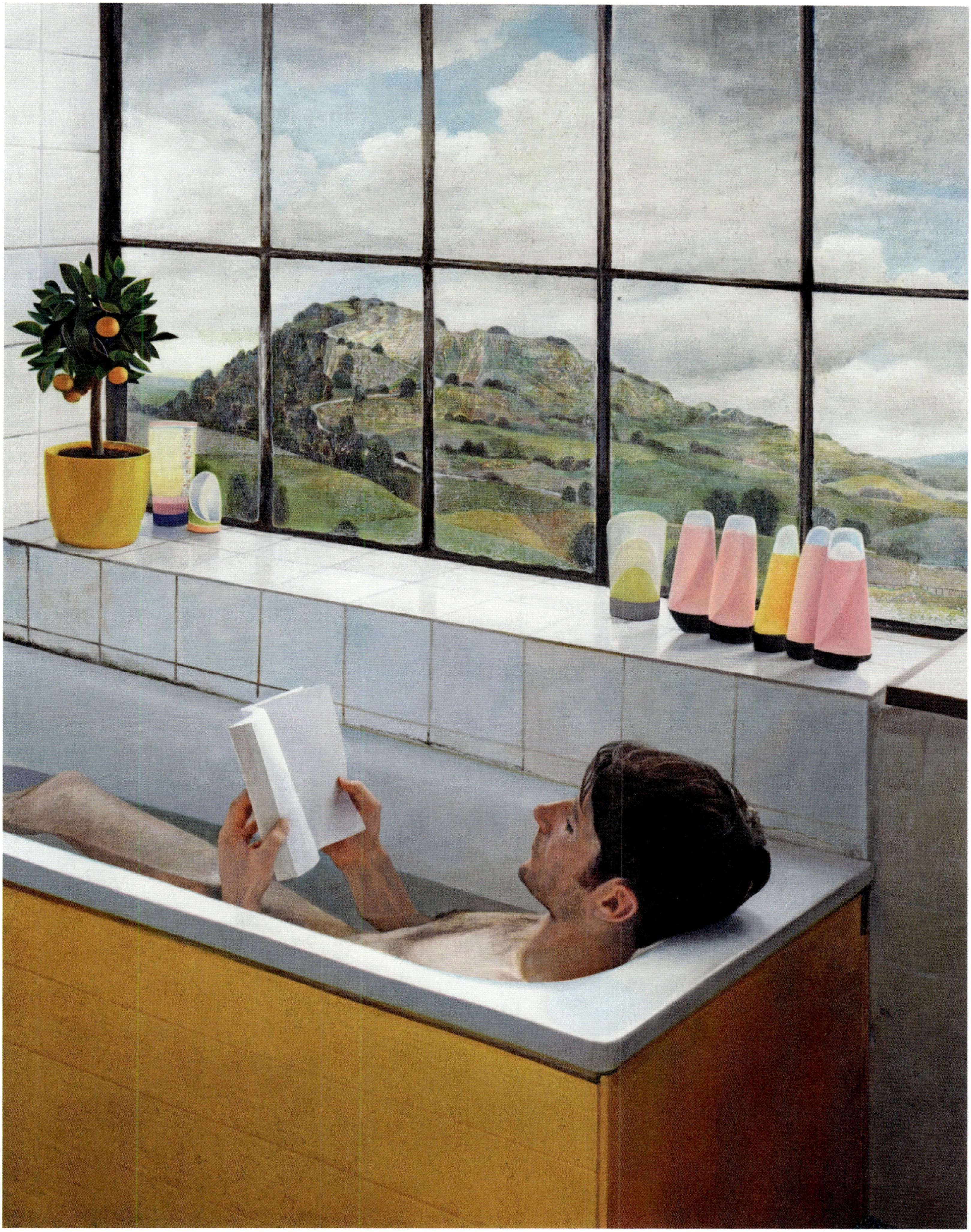

0. Gareth Cadwallader, *Bath*, 2015–16

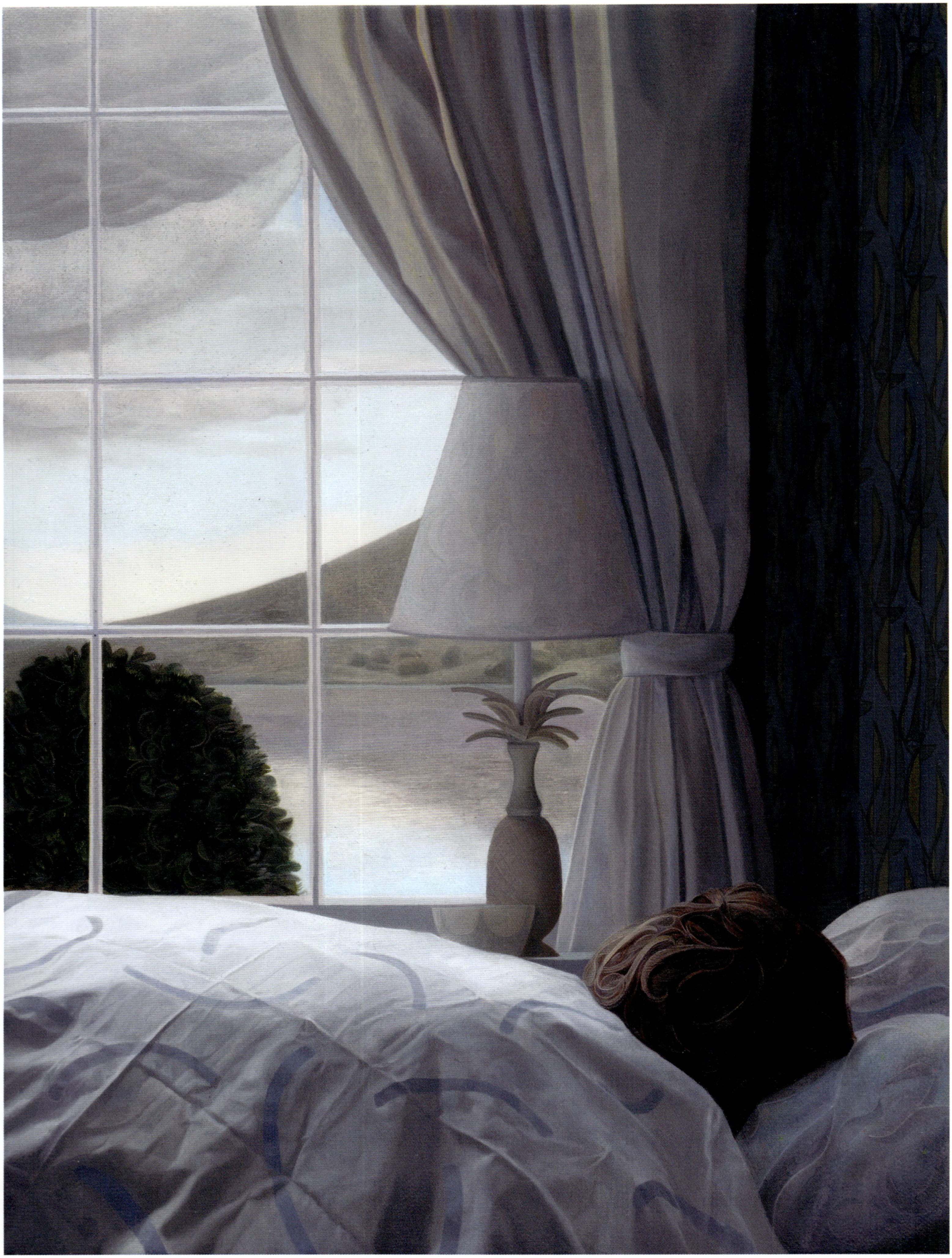

11. Gareth Cadwallader, *Bed*, 2017

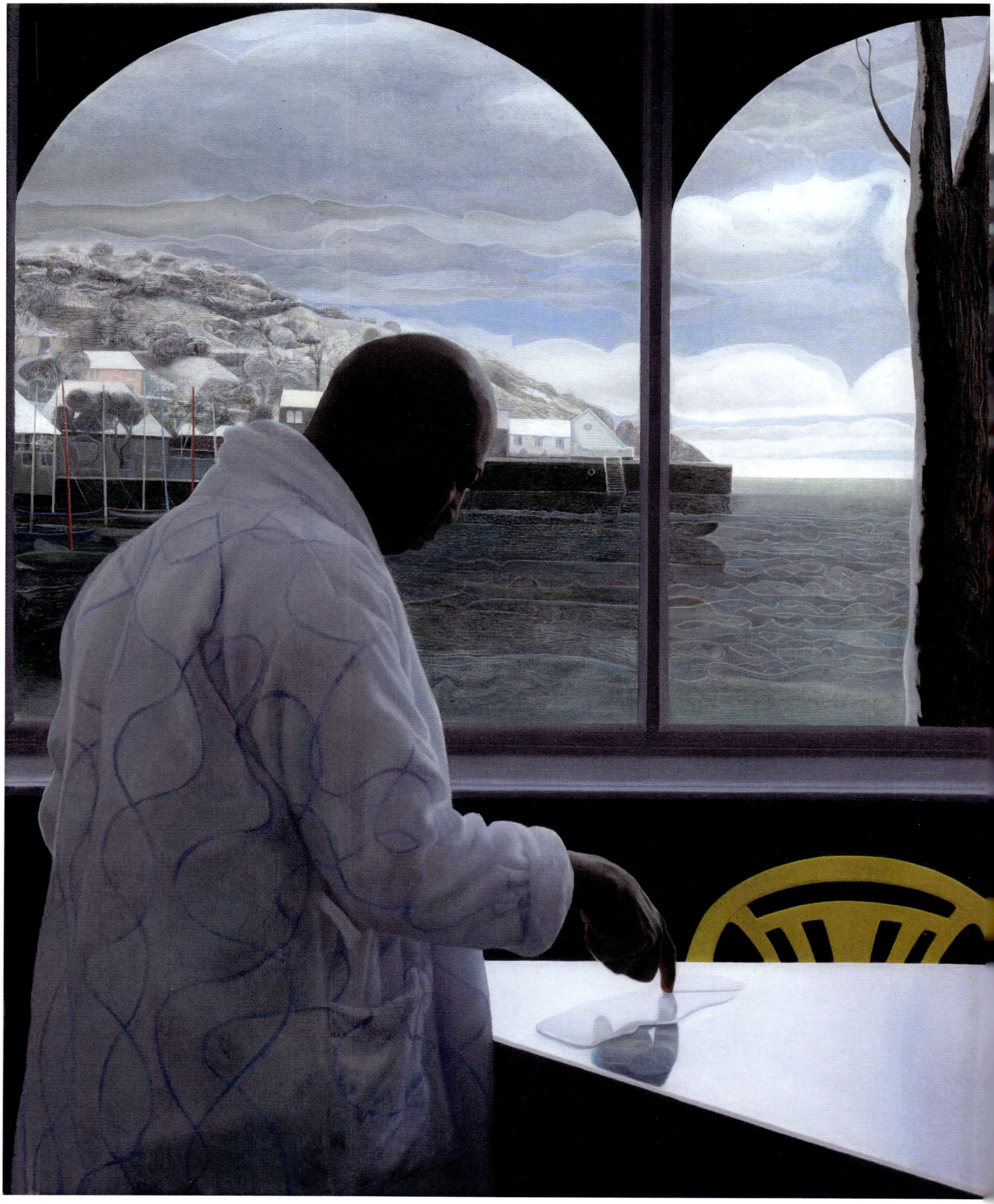

12. Gareth Cadwallader, *Milk*, 2017

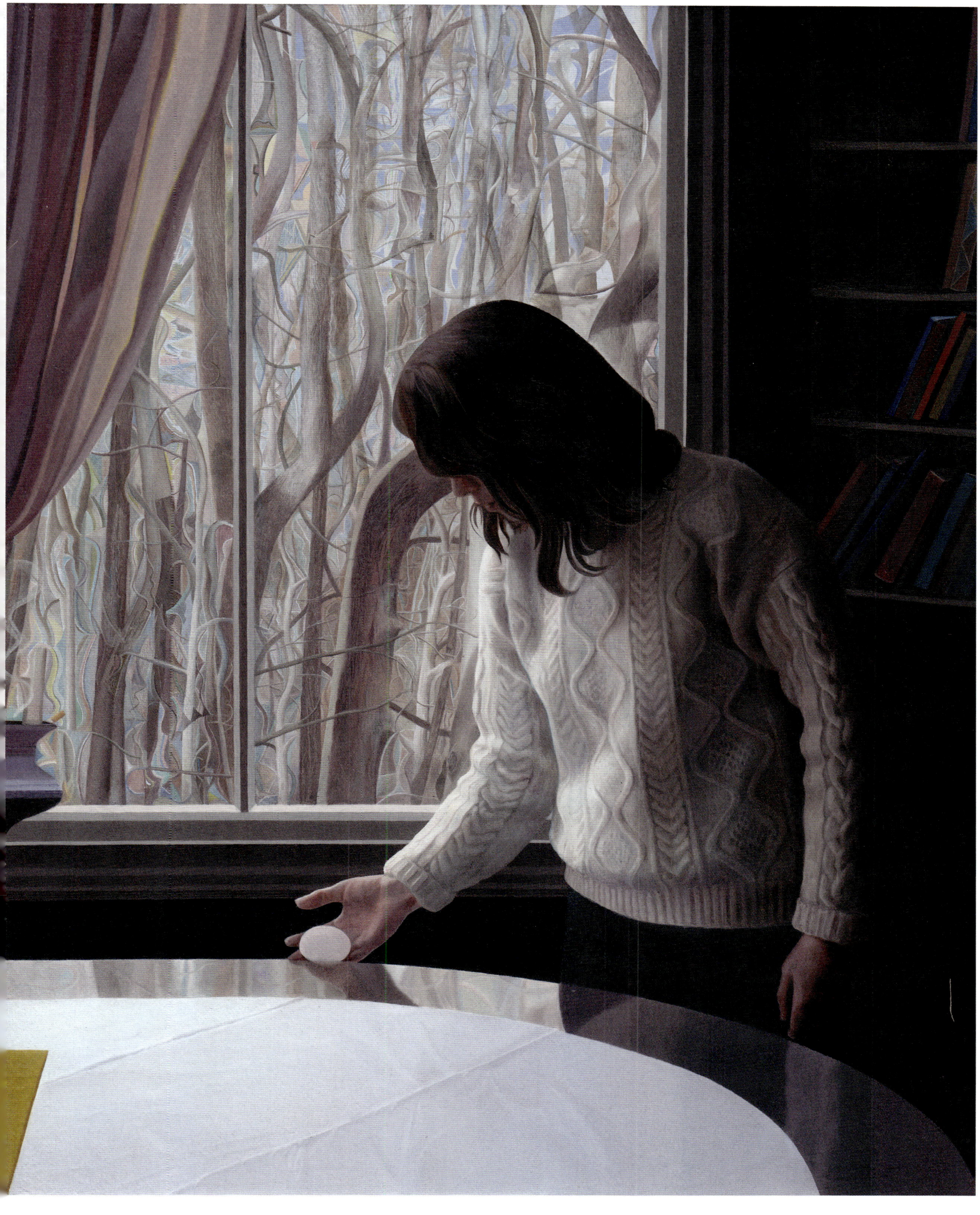

13. Gareth Cadwallader, *Egg*, 2018

VARDA CAIVANO

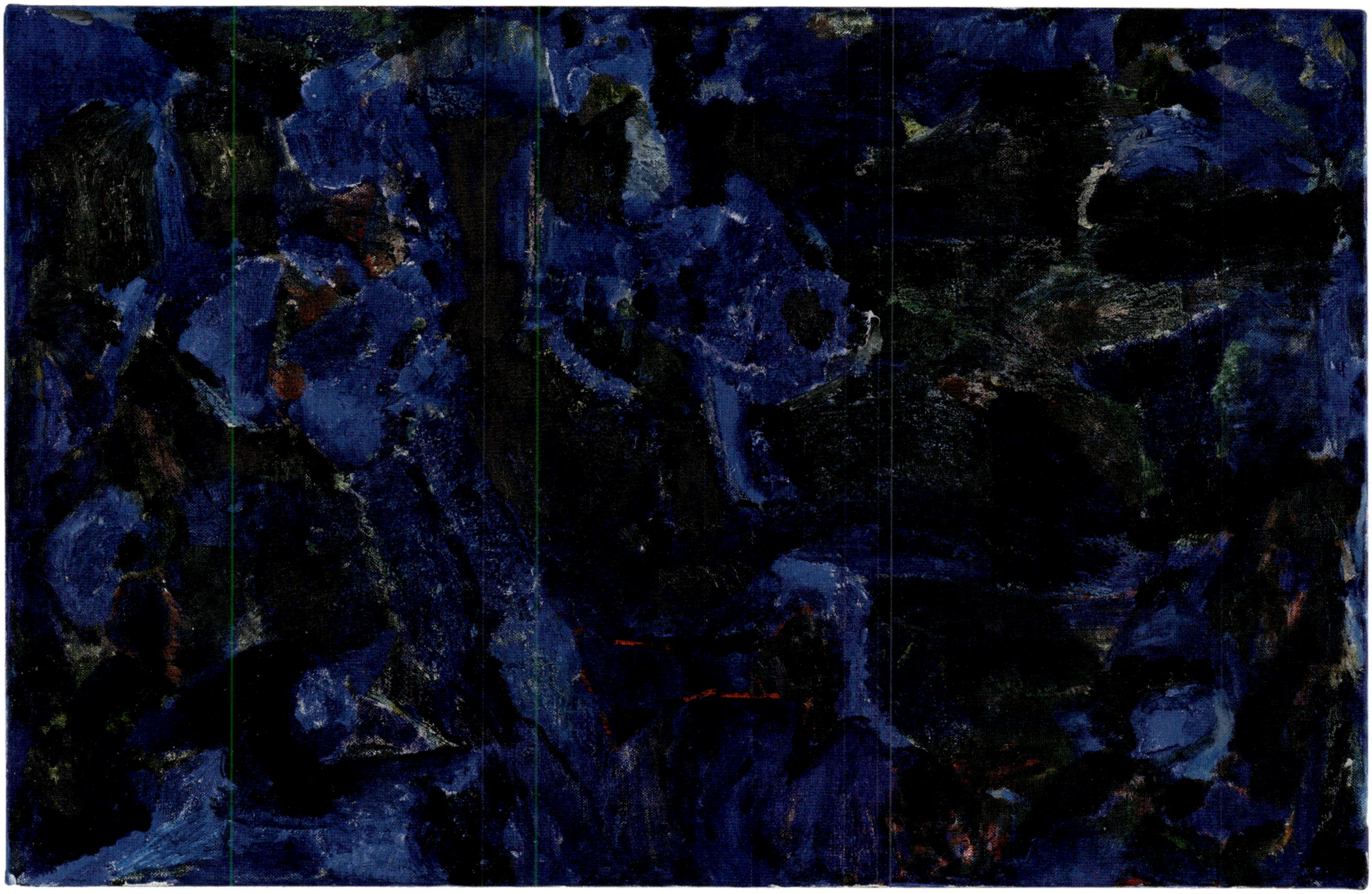

14. Varda Caivano, *Untitled*, 2011

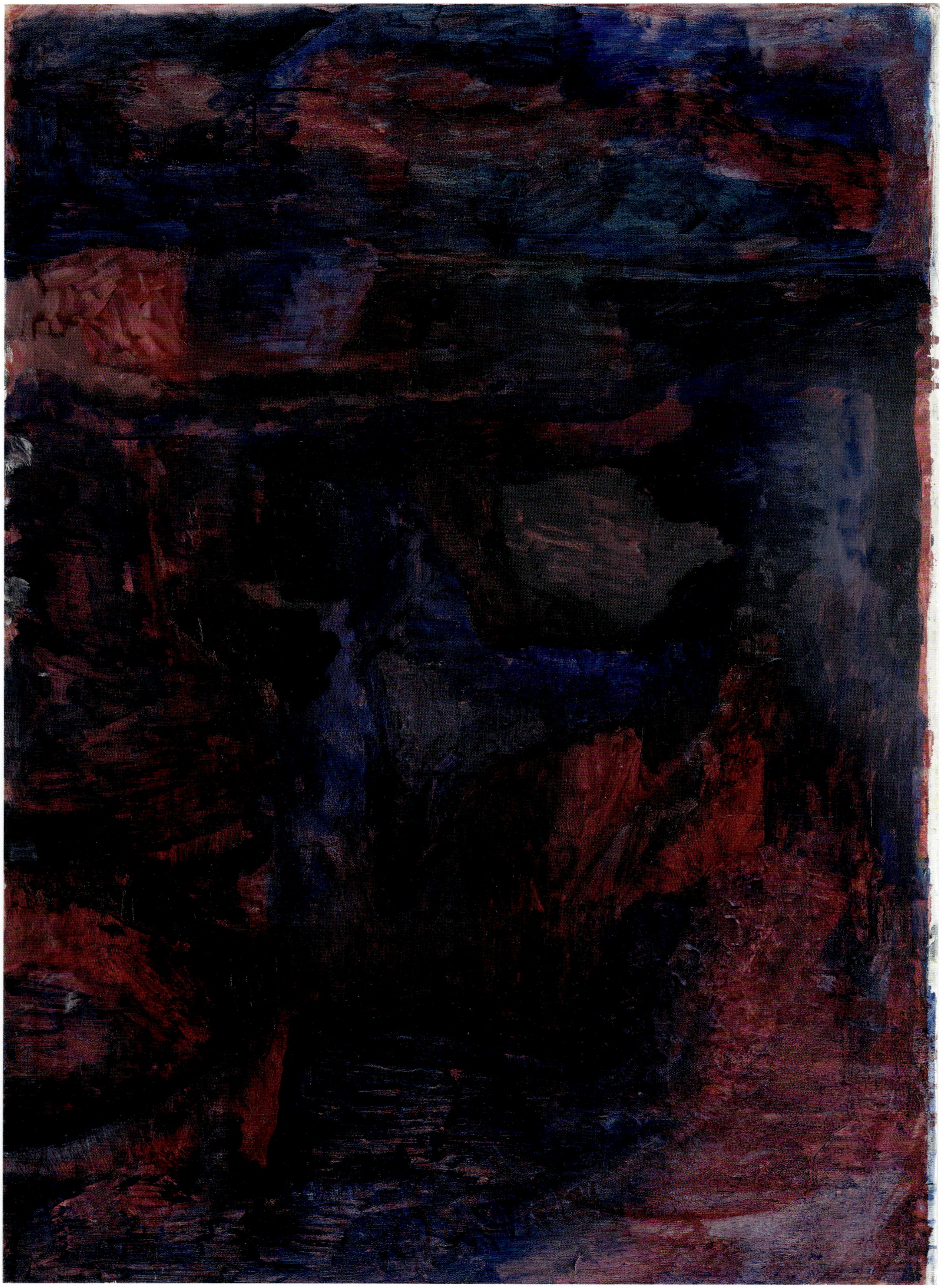

15. Varda Caivano, *Untitled*, 2018

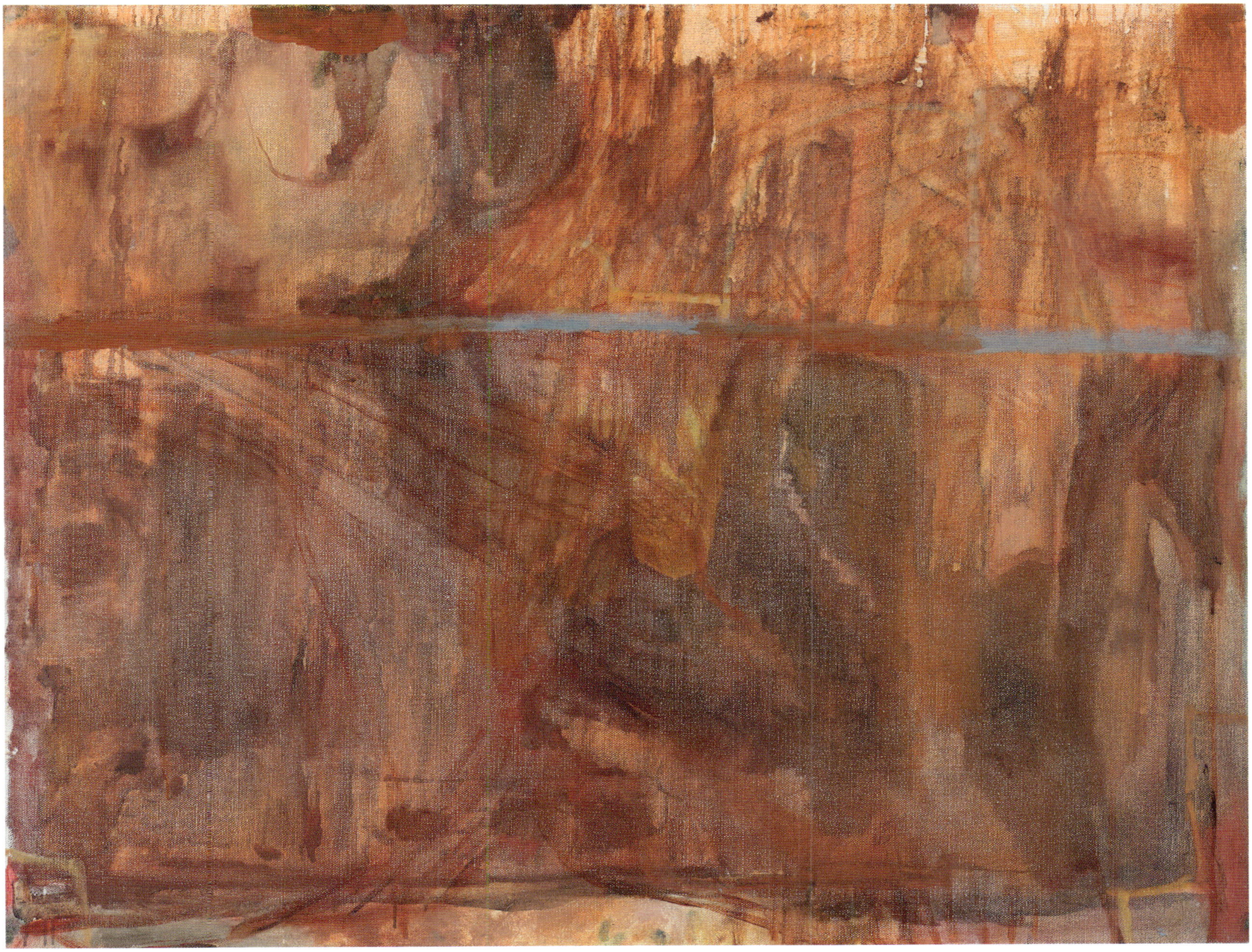

16. Varda Caivano, *Untitled*, 2012–18

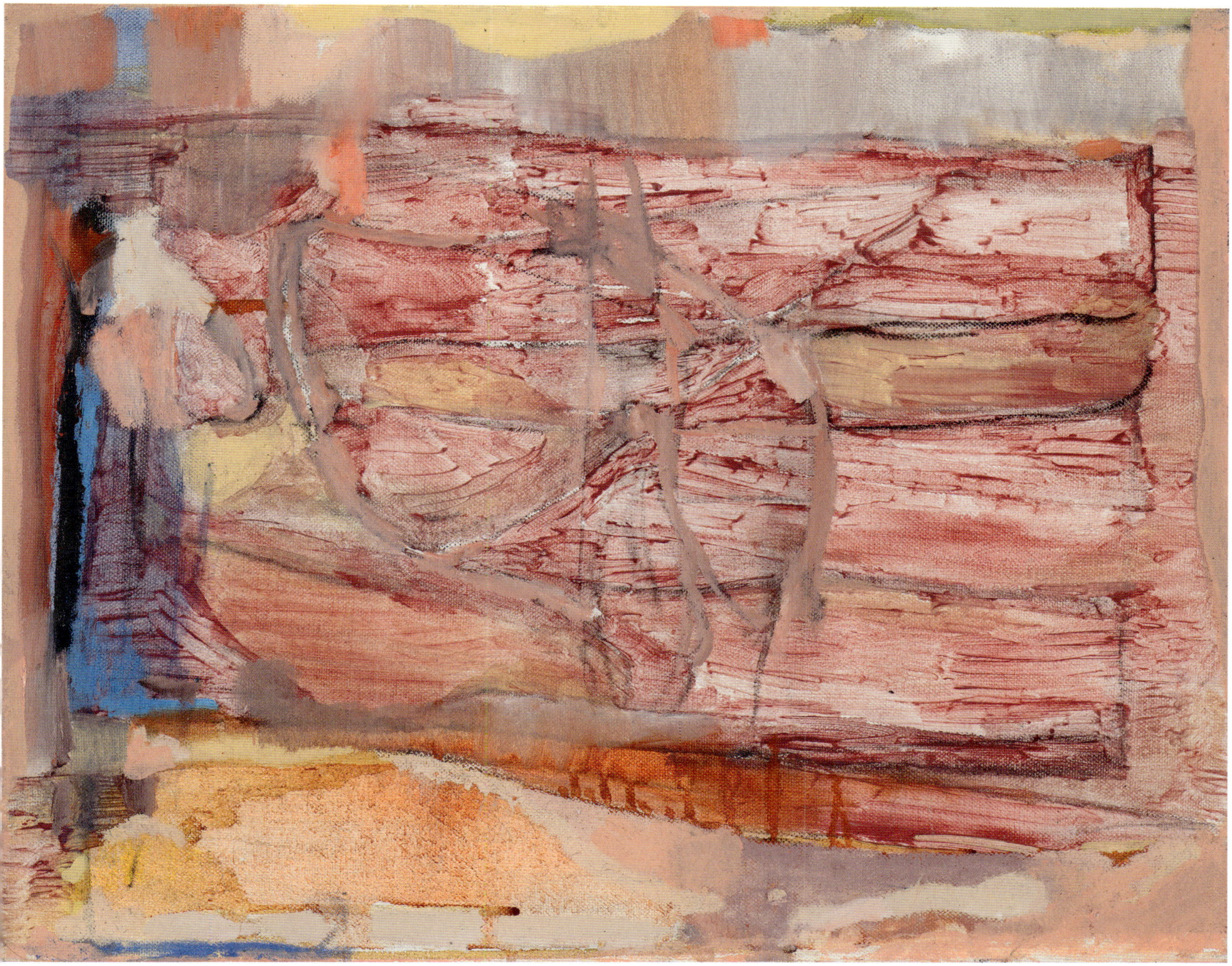

17. Varda Caivano, *Untitled*, 2018

LUBAINA HIMID

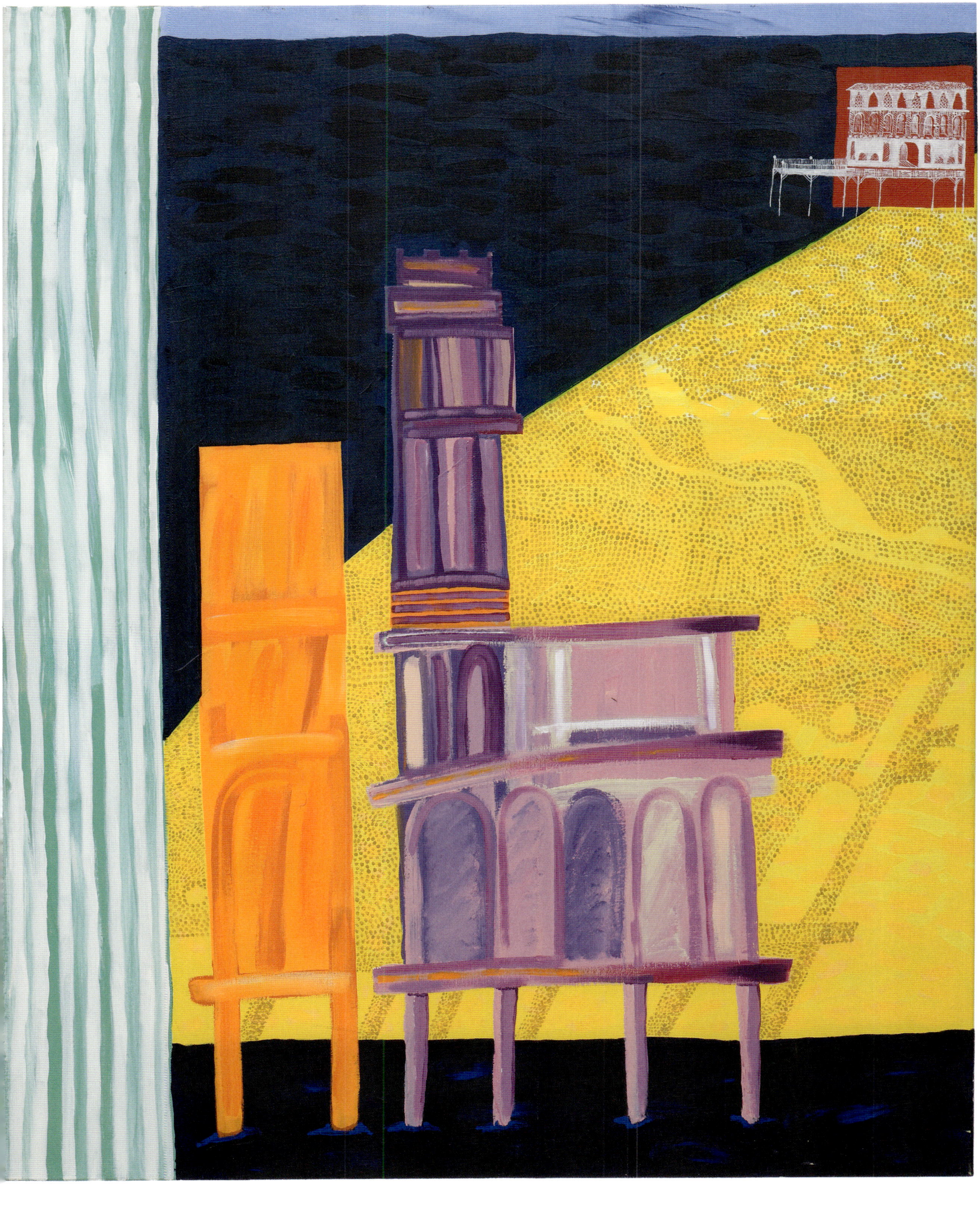

18. Lubaina Himid, *Garfoni*, 1995

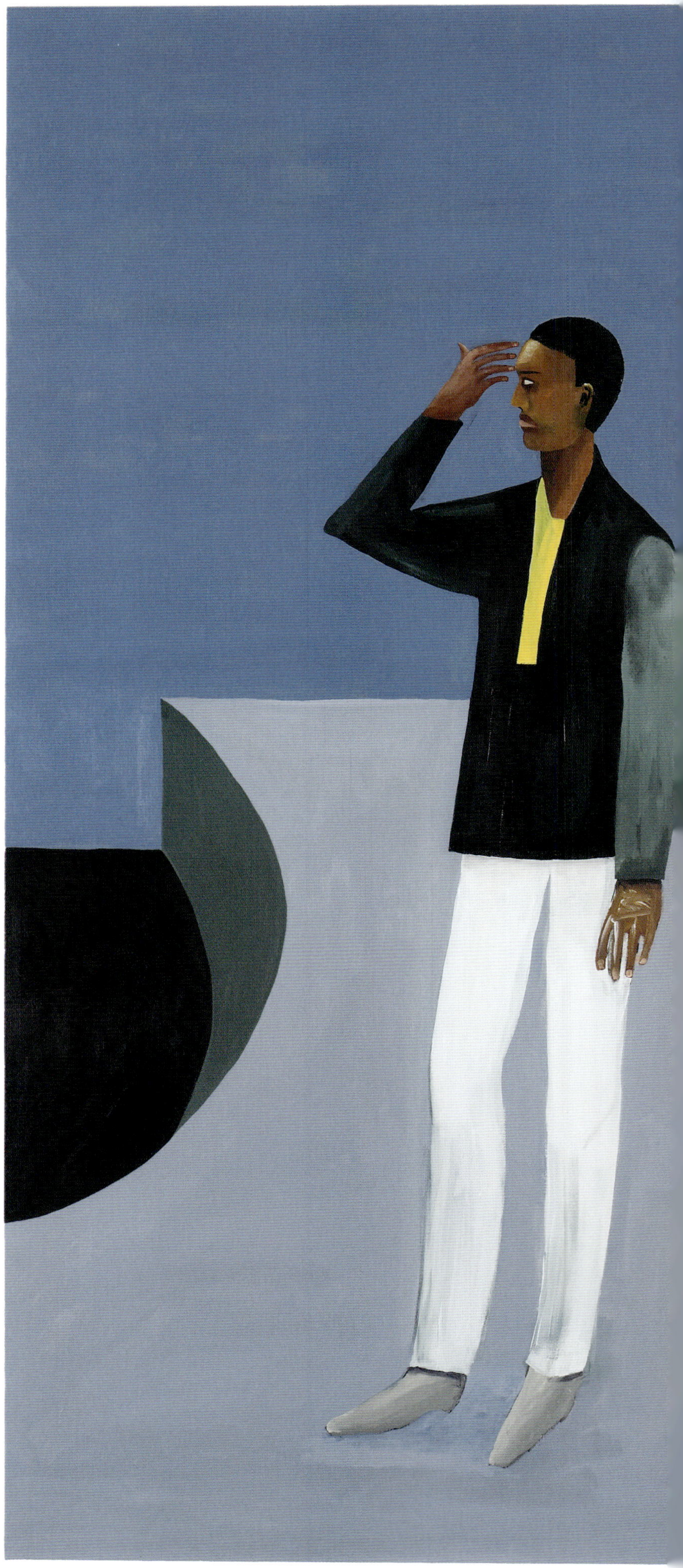

19. Lubaina Himid, *Le Rodeur: The Exchange*, 2016

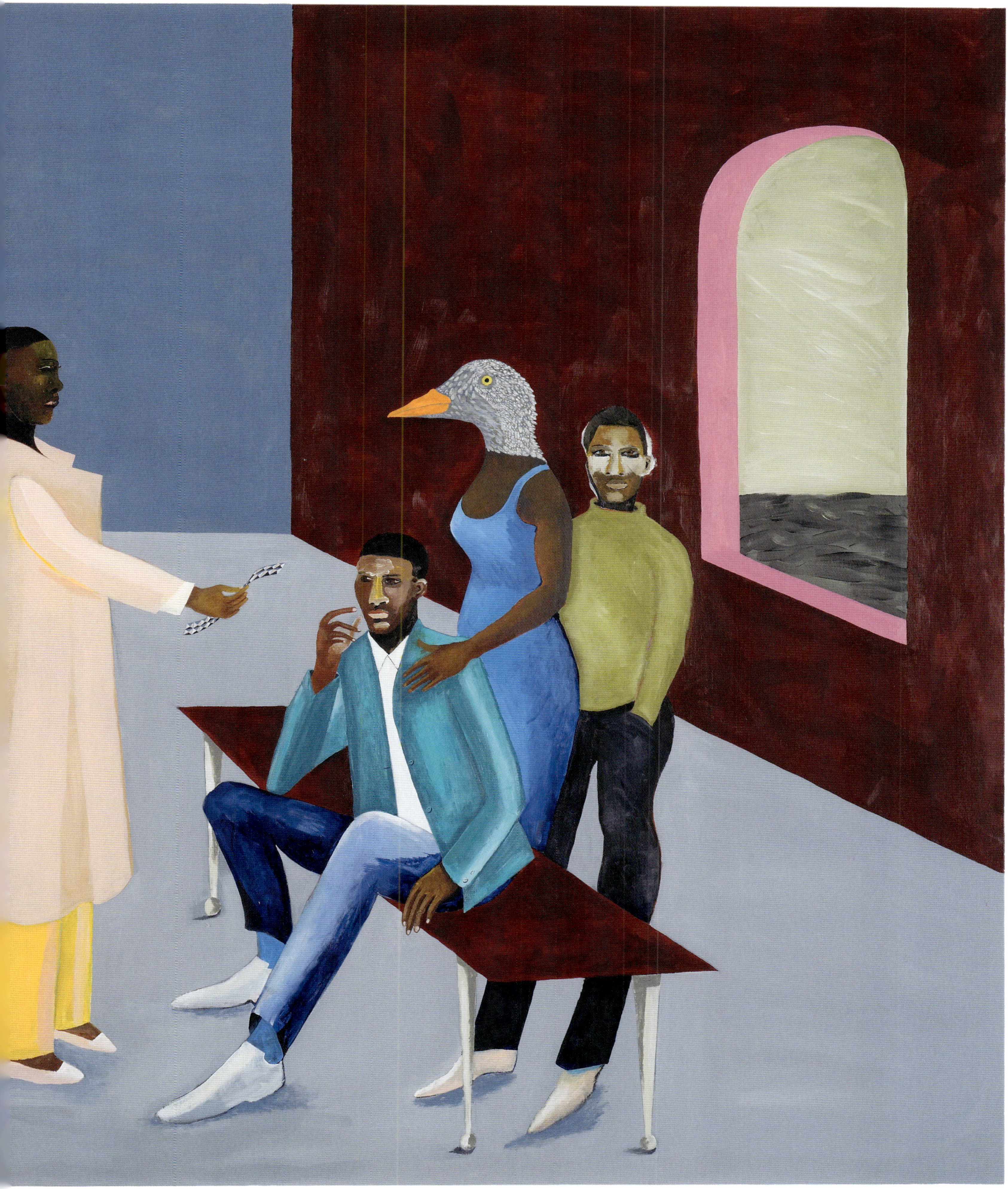

PAUL HOUSLEY

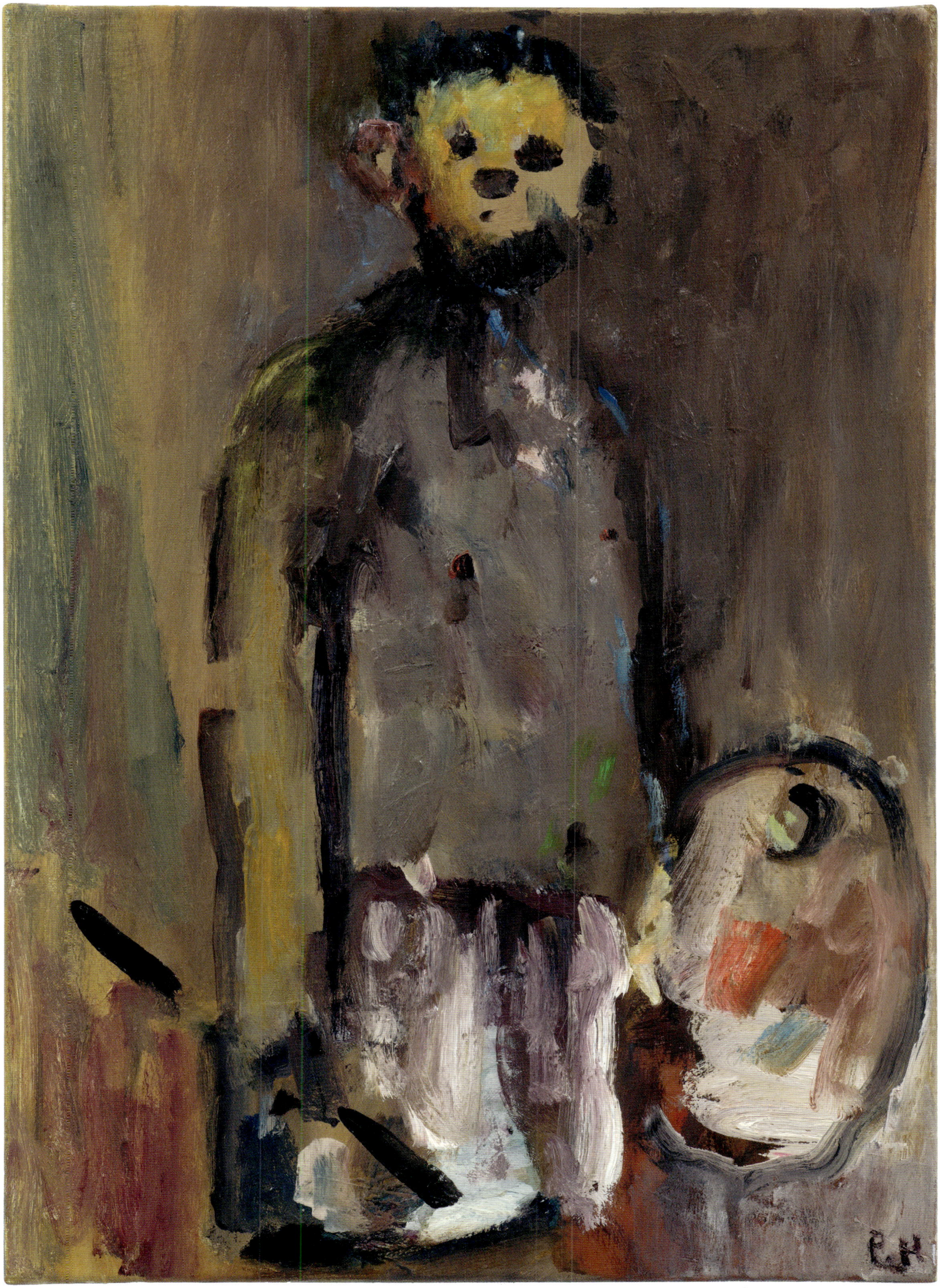

20. Paul Housley, *Grey Monarch*, 2019

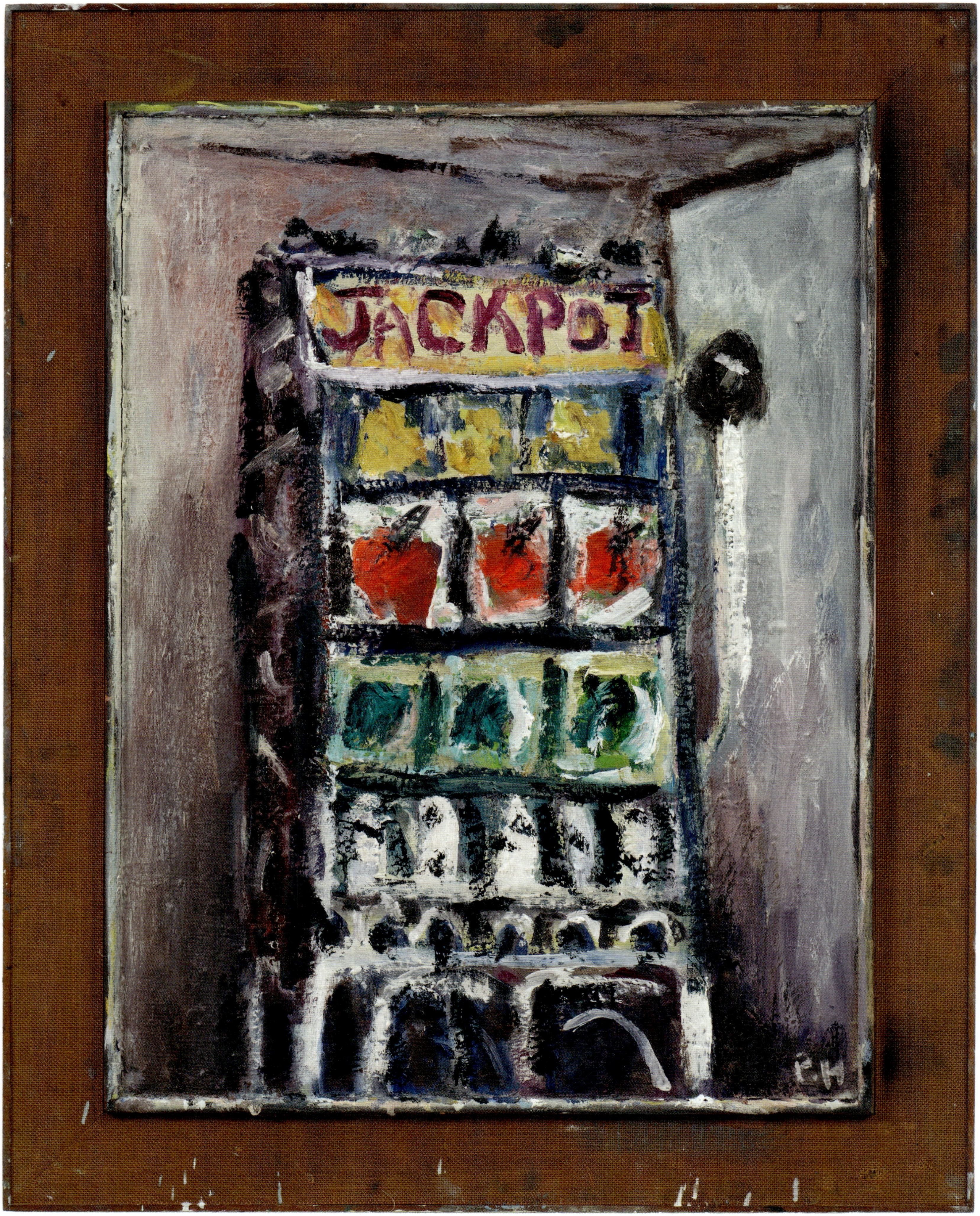

21. Paul Housley, *Prizes for Creeps*, 2019

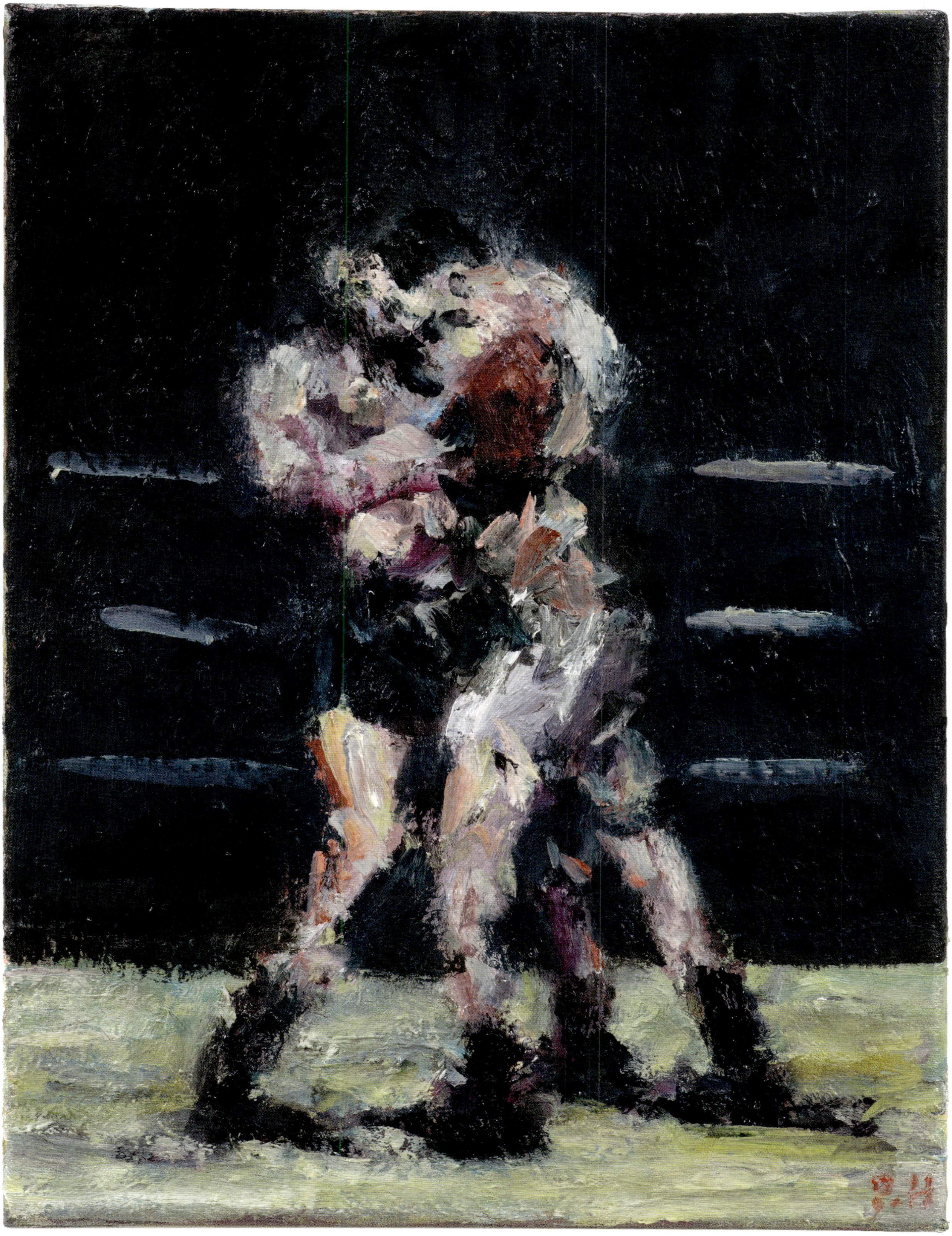

22. Paul Housley, *Slow Dance in the Long Game*, 2019

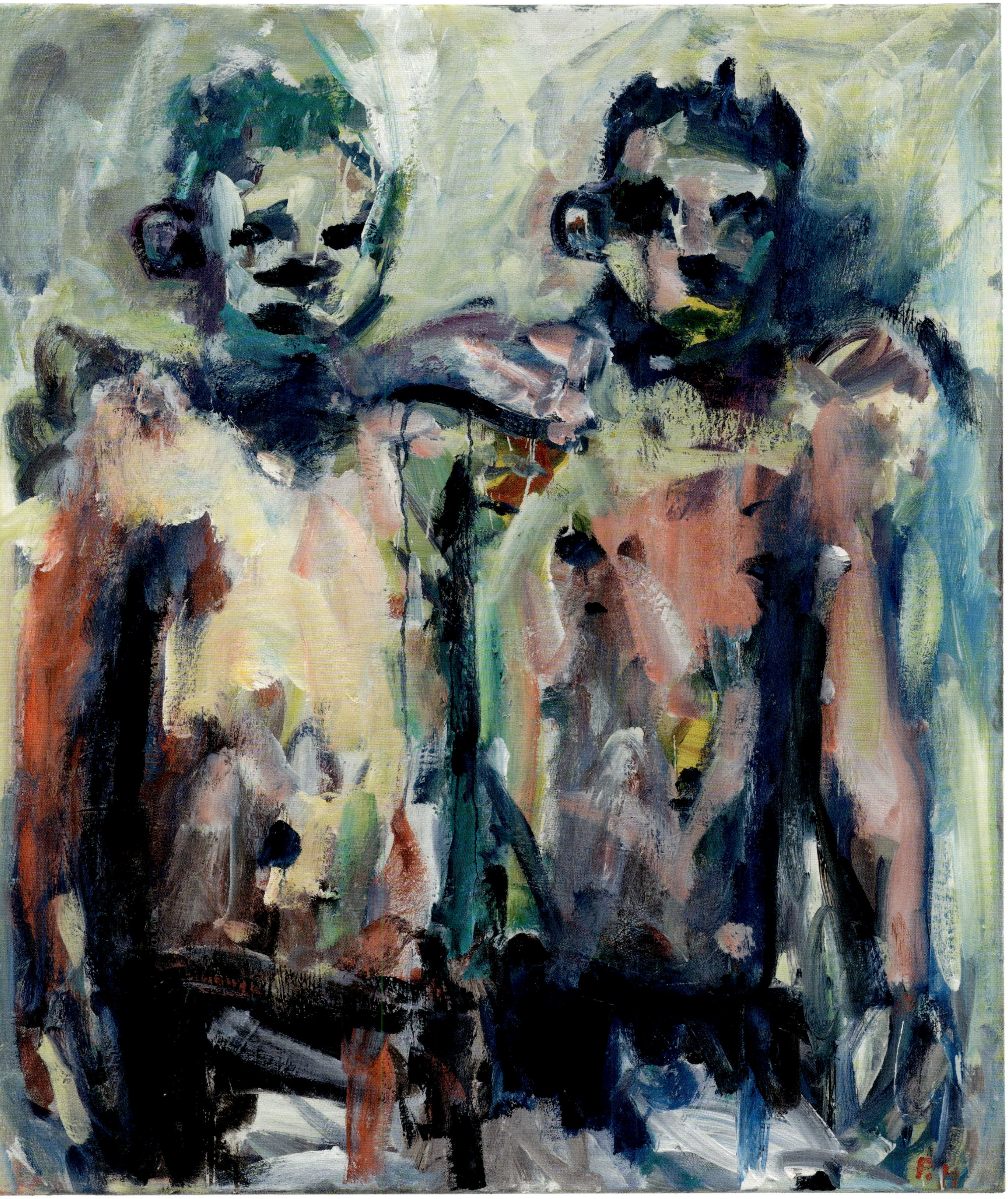

23. Paul Housley, *Two Painters*, 2019

MERLIN JAMES

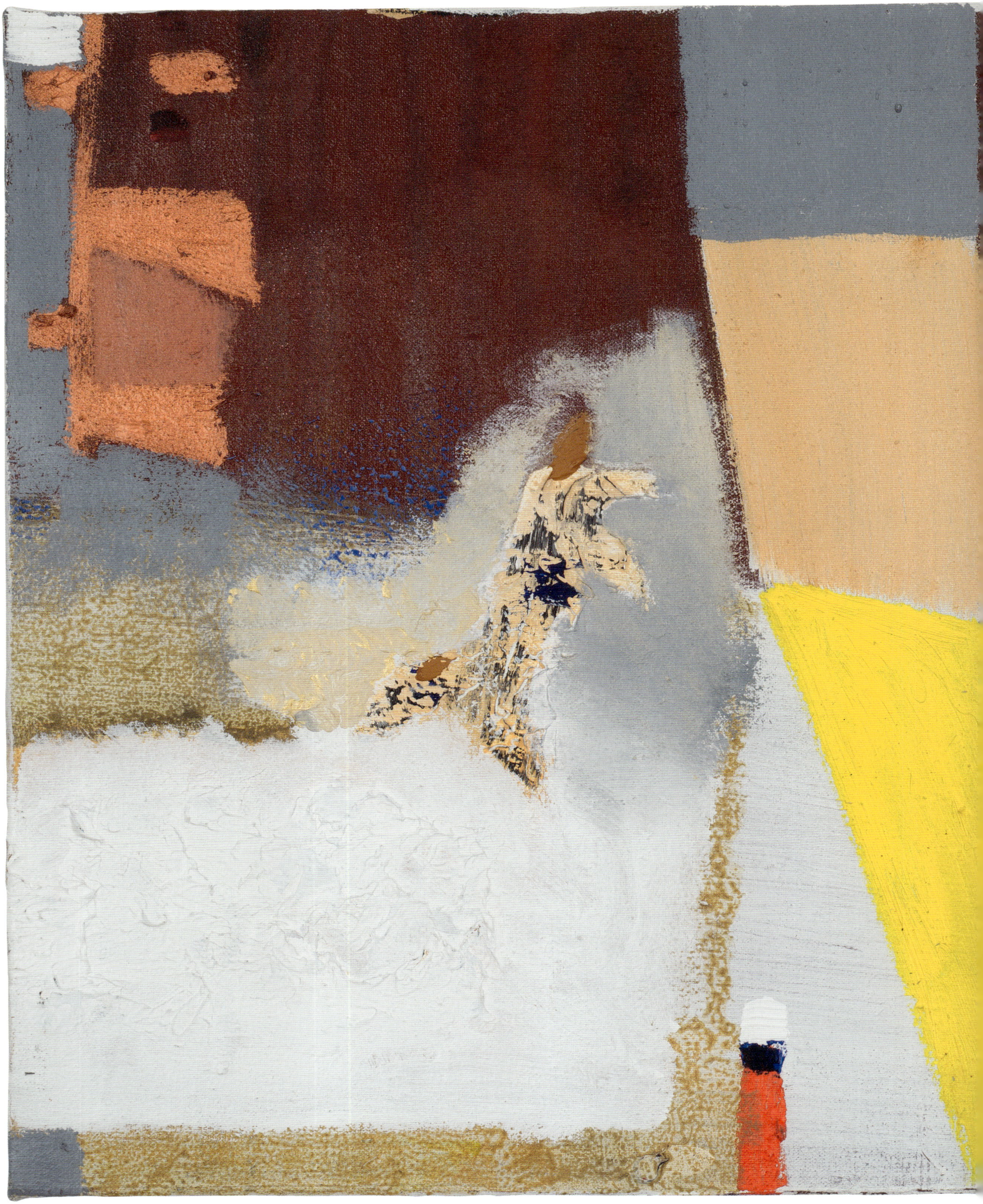

24. Merlin James, *Chien*, 2006–10

25. Merlin James, *Hanger*, 2016

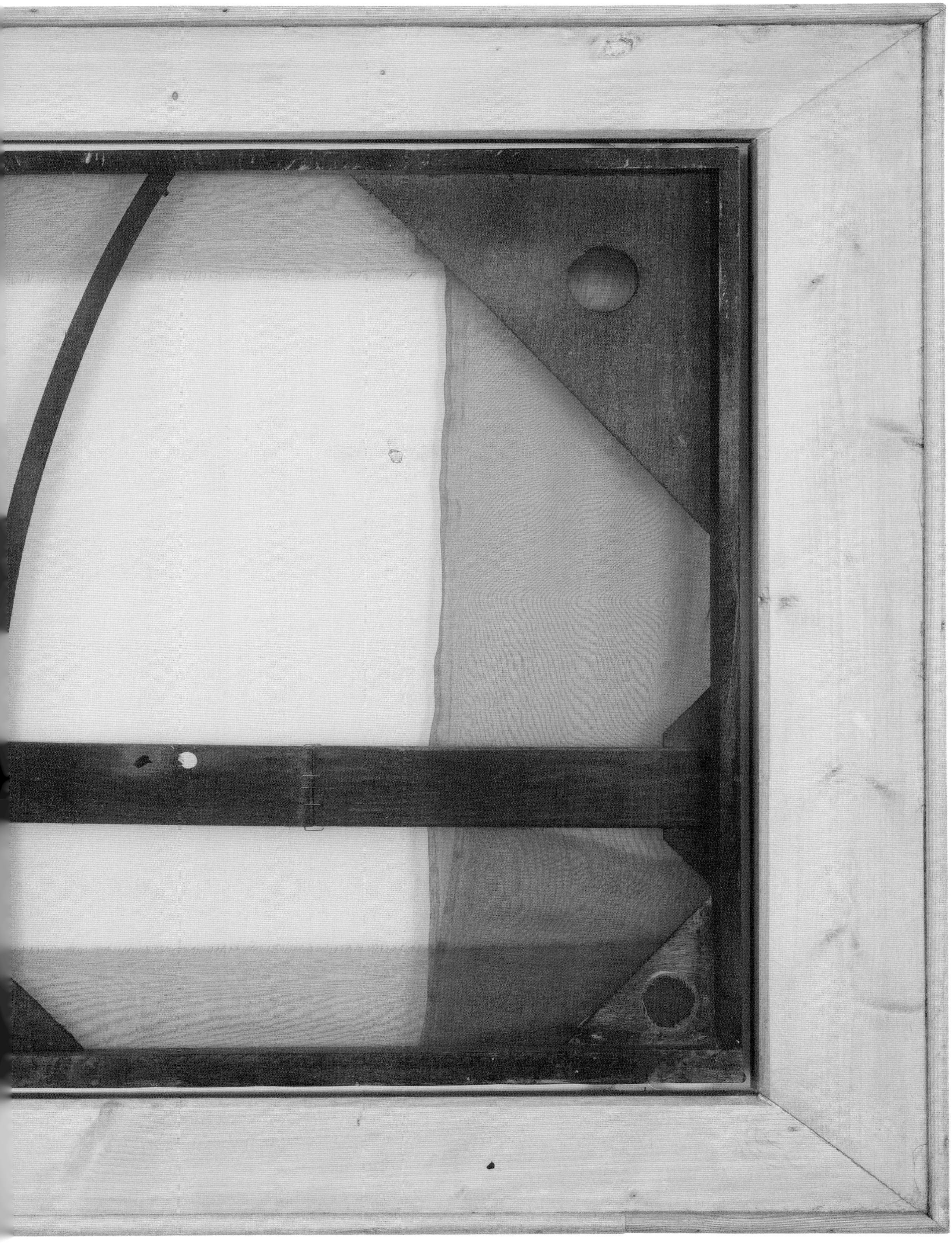

26. Merlin James, *Mirror*, 2019

27. Merlin James, *Bay*, 1998

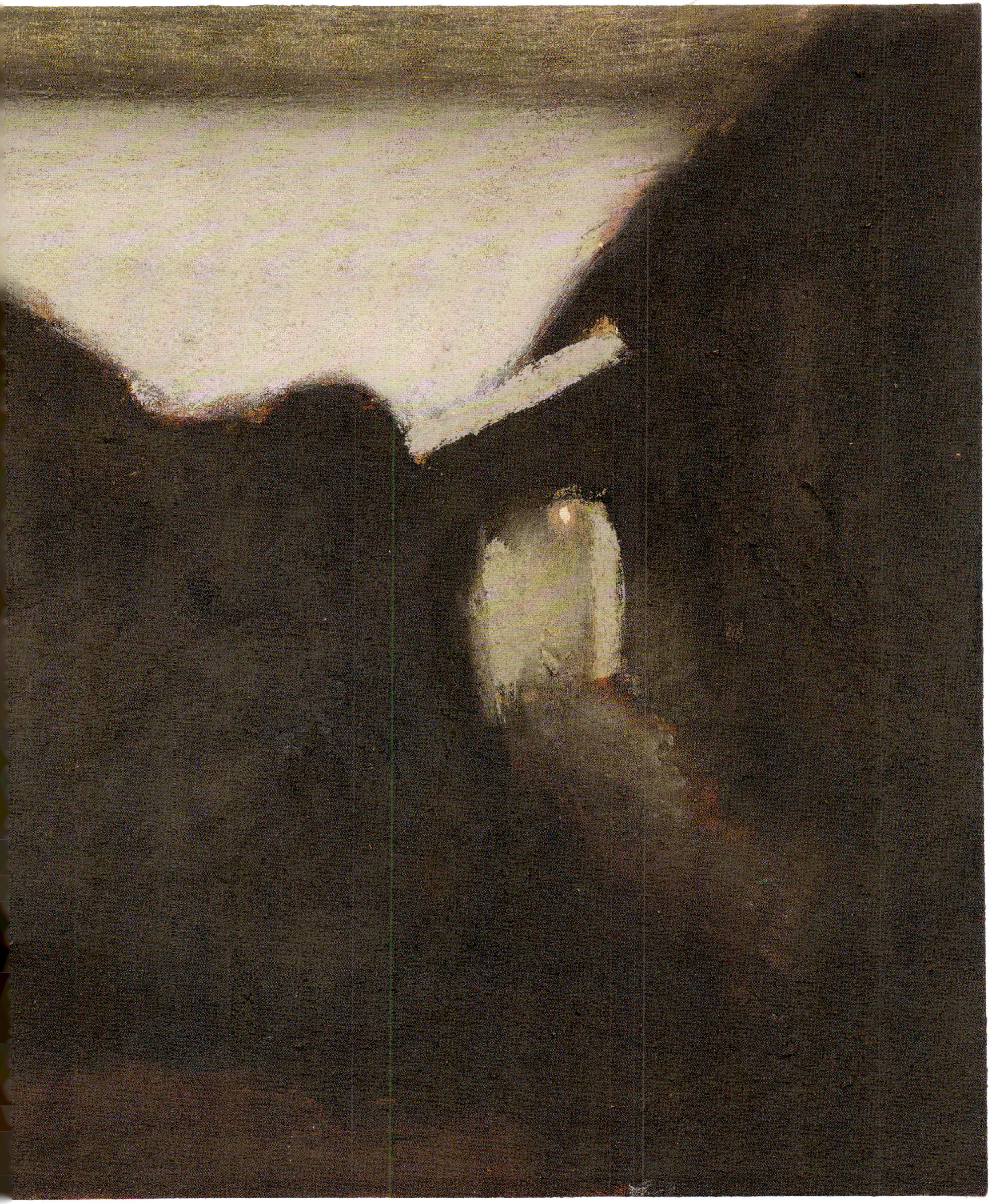

ALLISON KATZ

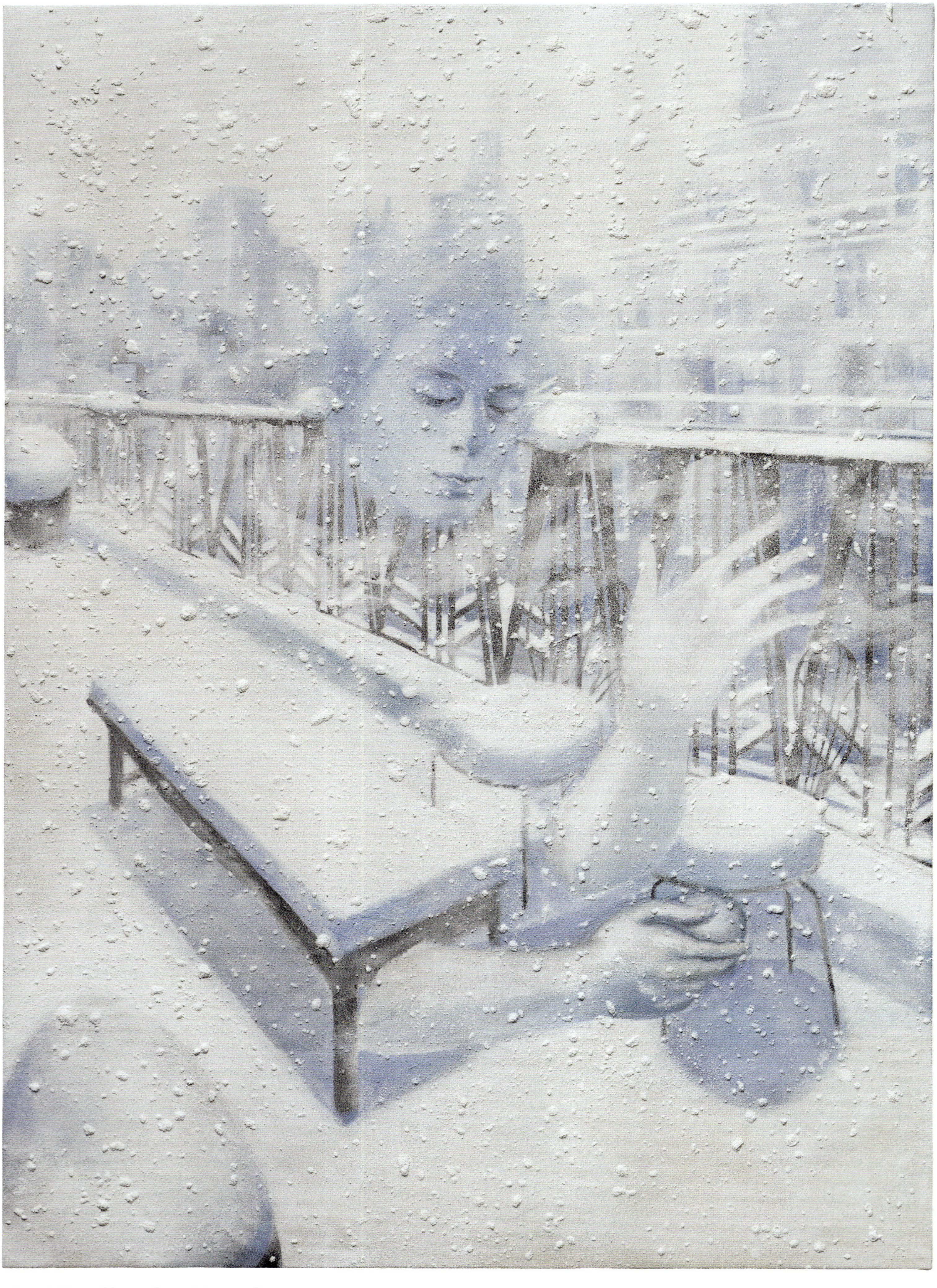

28. Allison Katz, *Snowglobe*, 2018

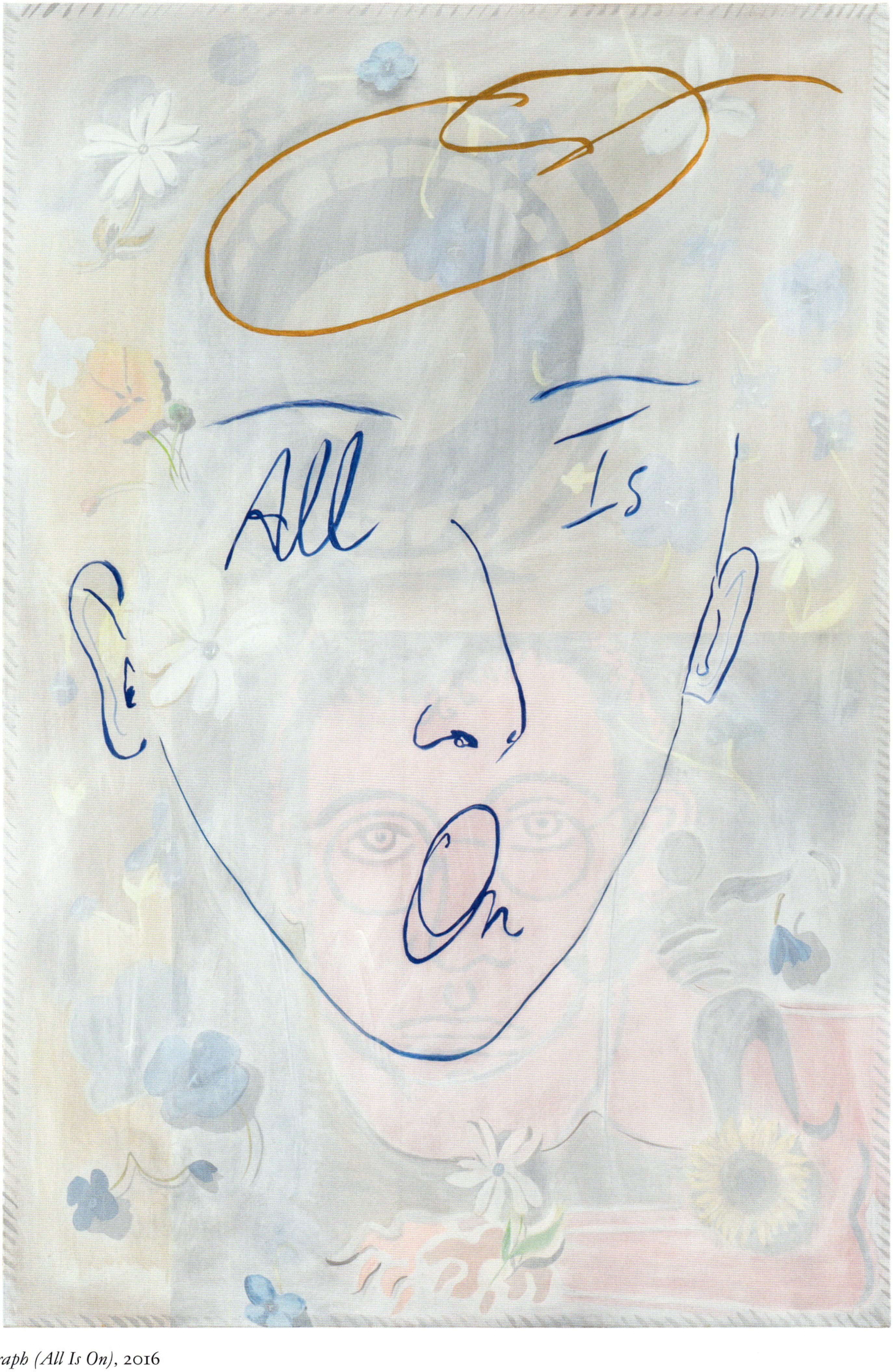

29. Allison Katz, *AKgraph (All Is On)*, 2016

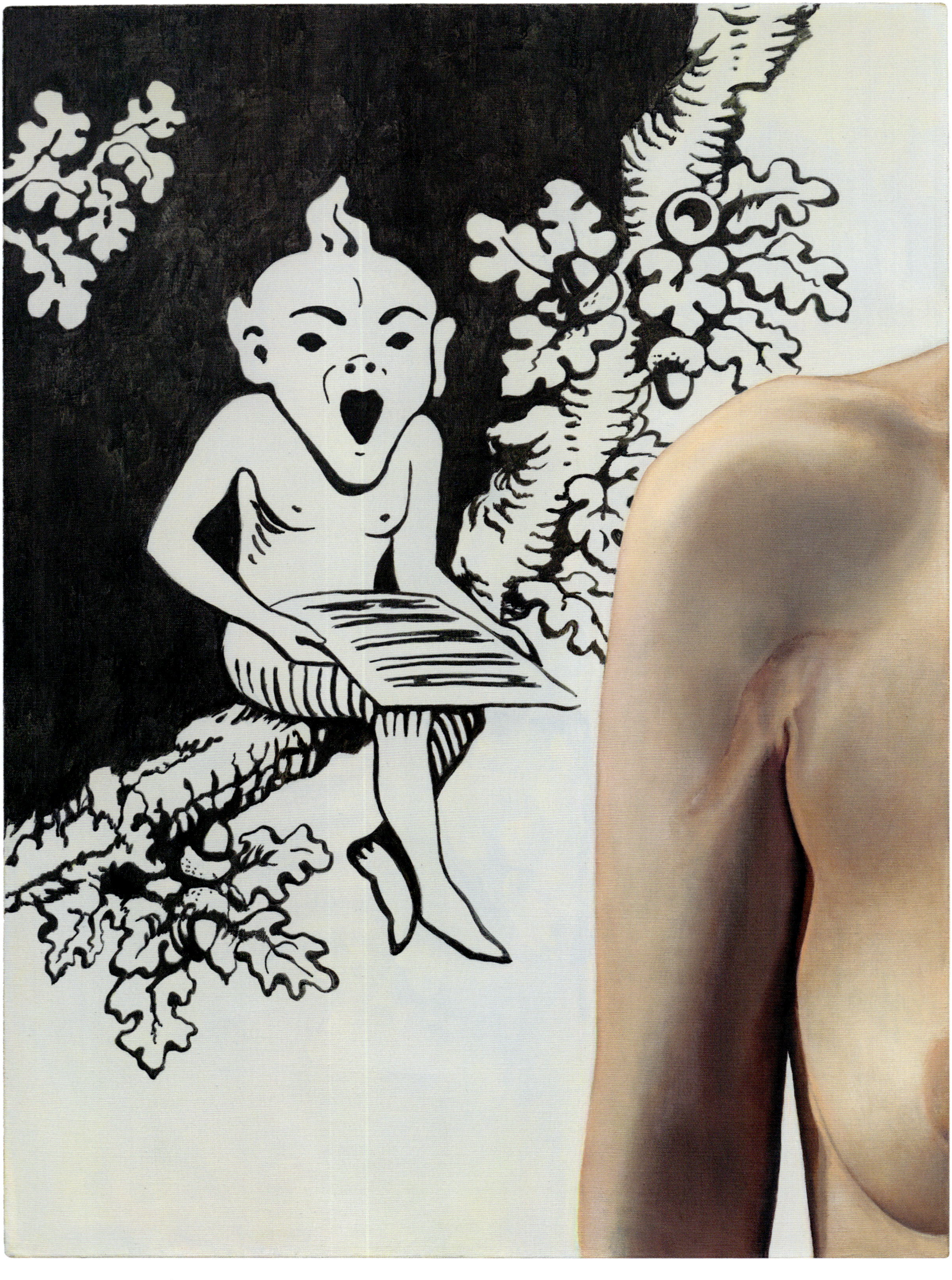

30. Allison Katz, *Elf-Esteem*, 2017

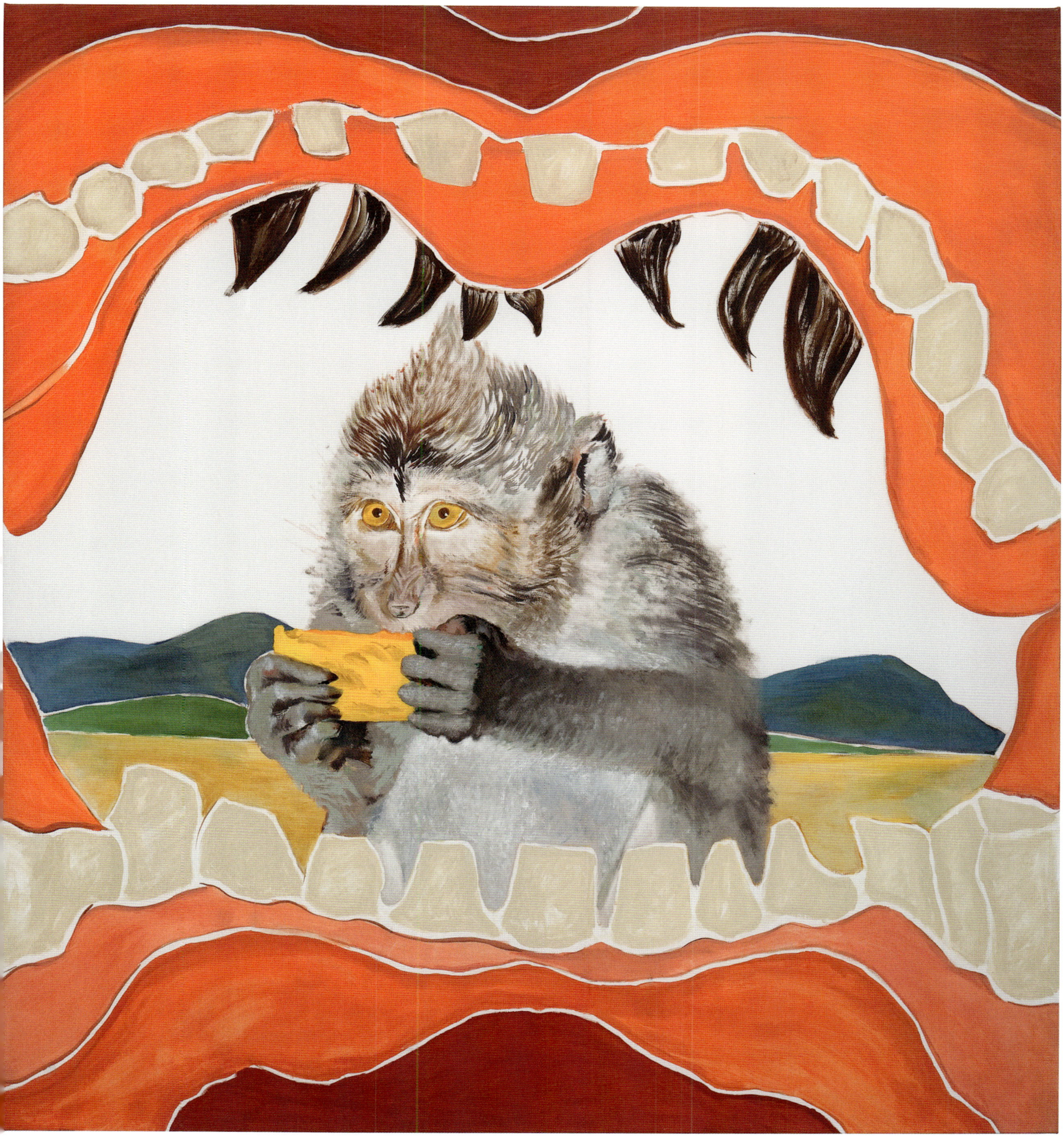

31. Allison Katz, *Double Hunger*, 2015

SIMON LING

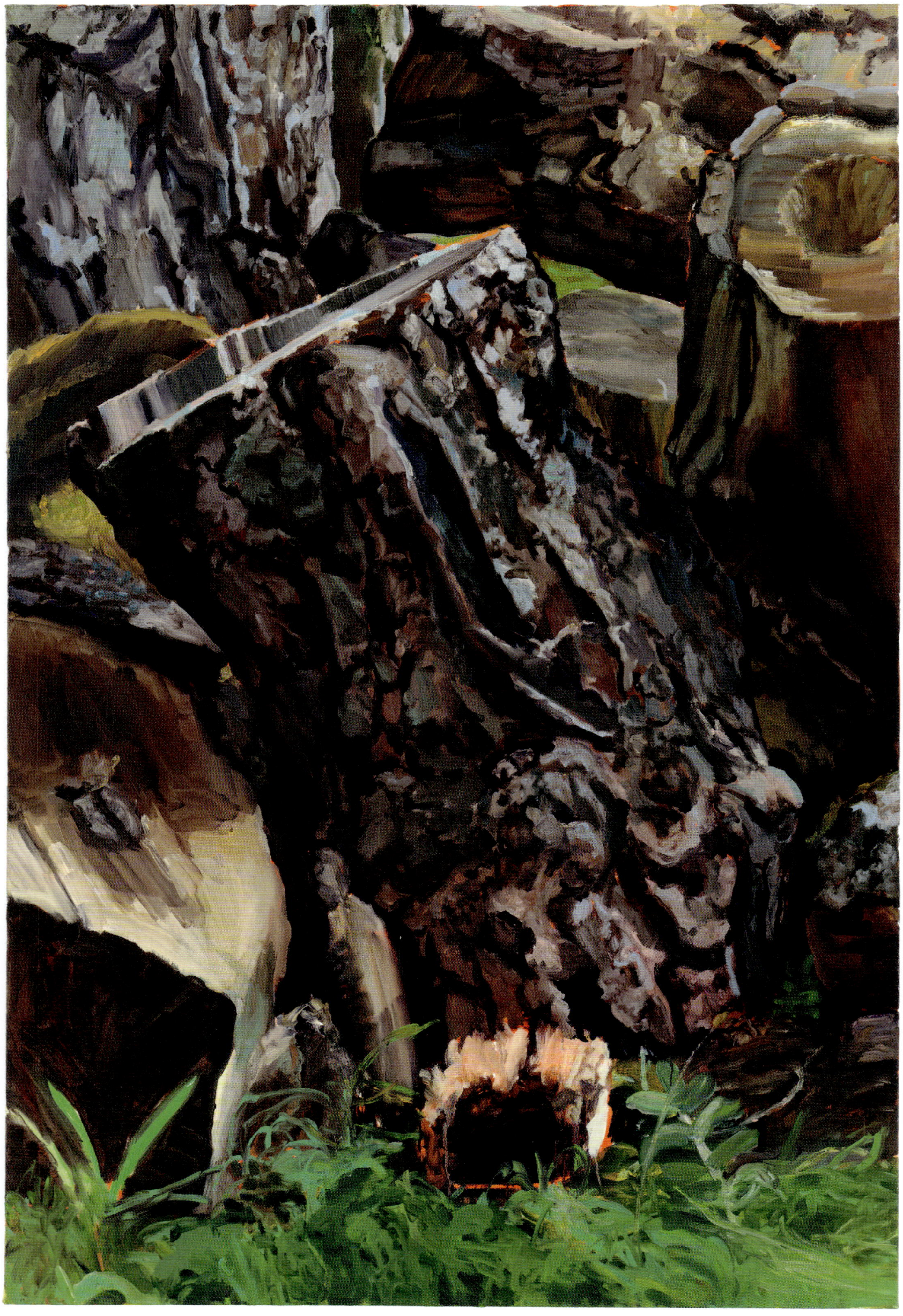

32. Simon Ling, *Untitled*, 2016

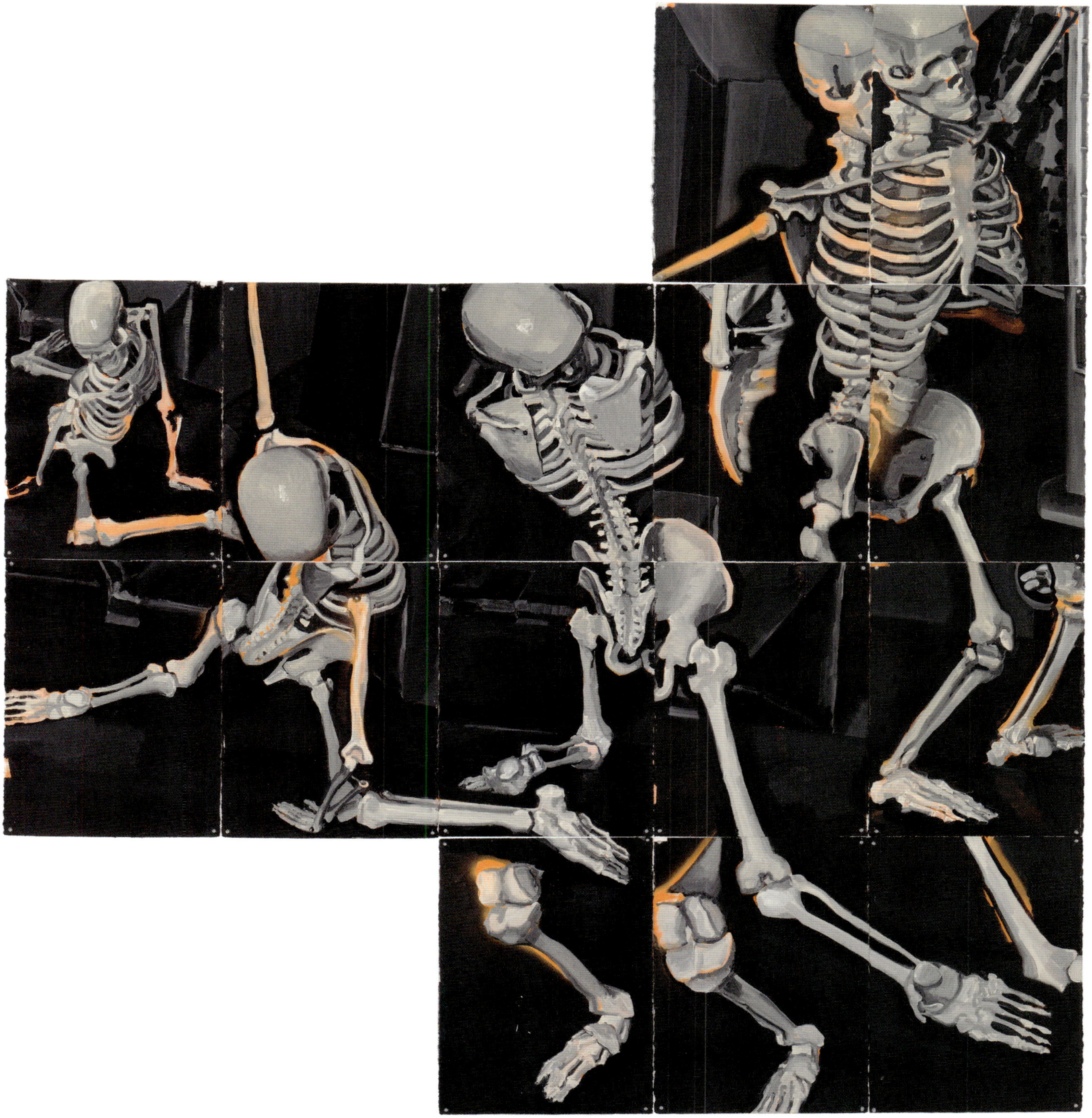

33. Simon Ling, *Untitled*, 2018

LUCY MCKENZIE

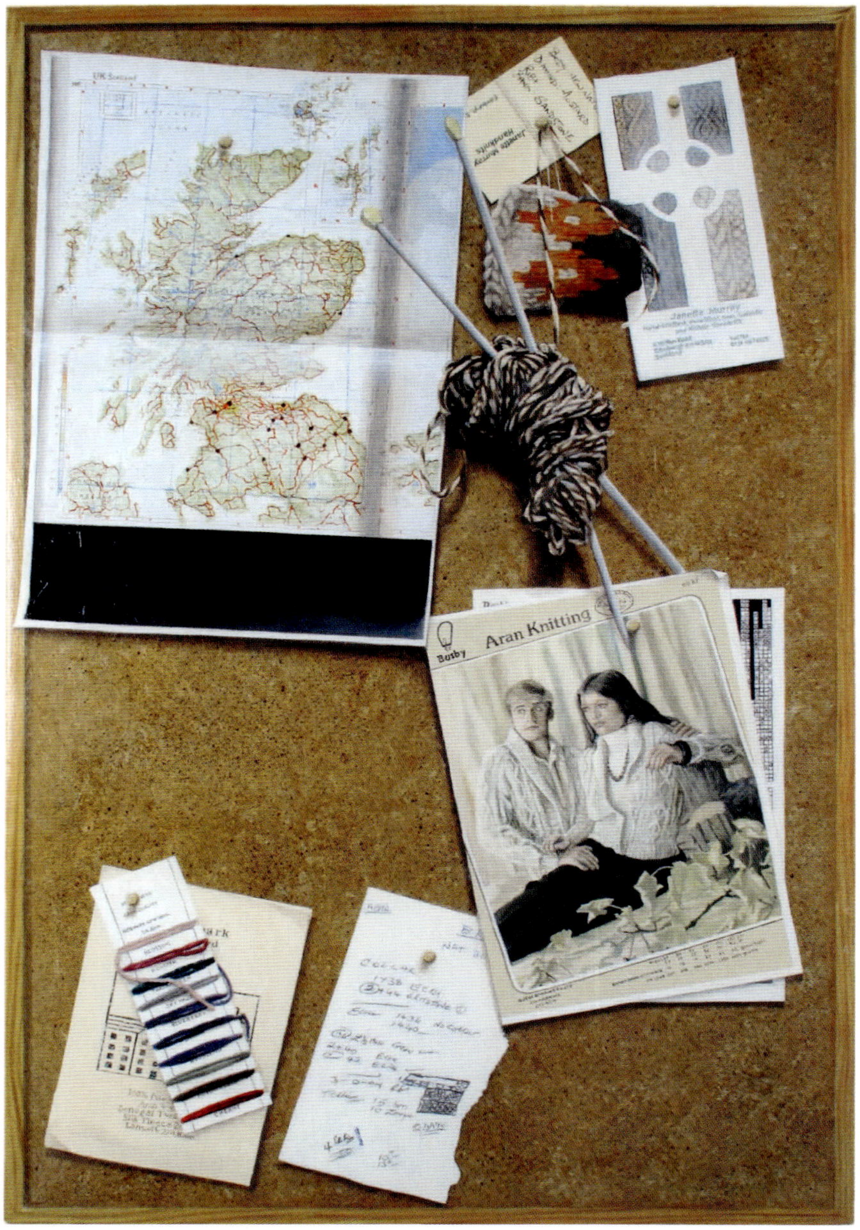

34. Lucy McKenzie, *Quodlibet XI (Janette Murray)*, 2011

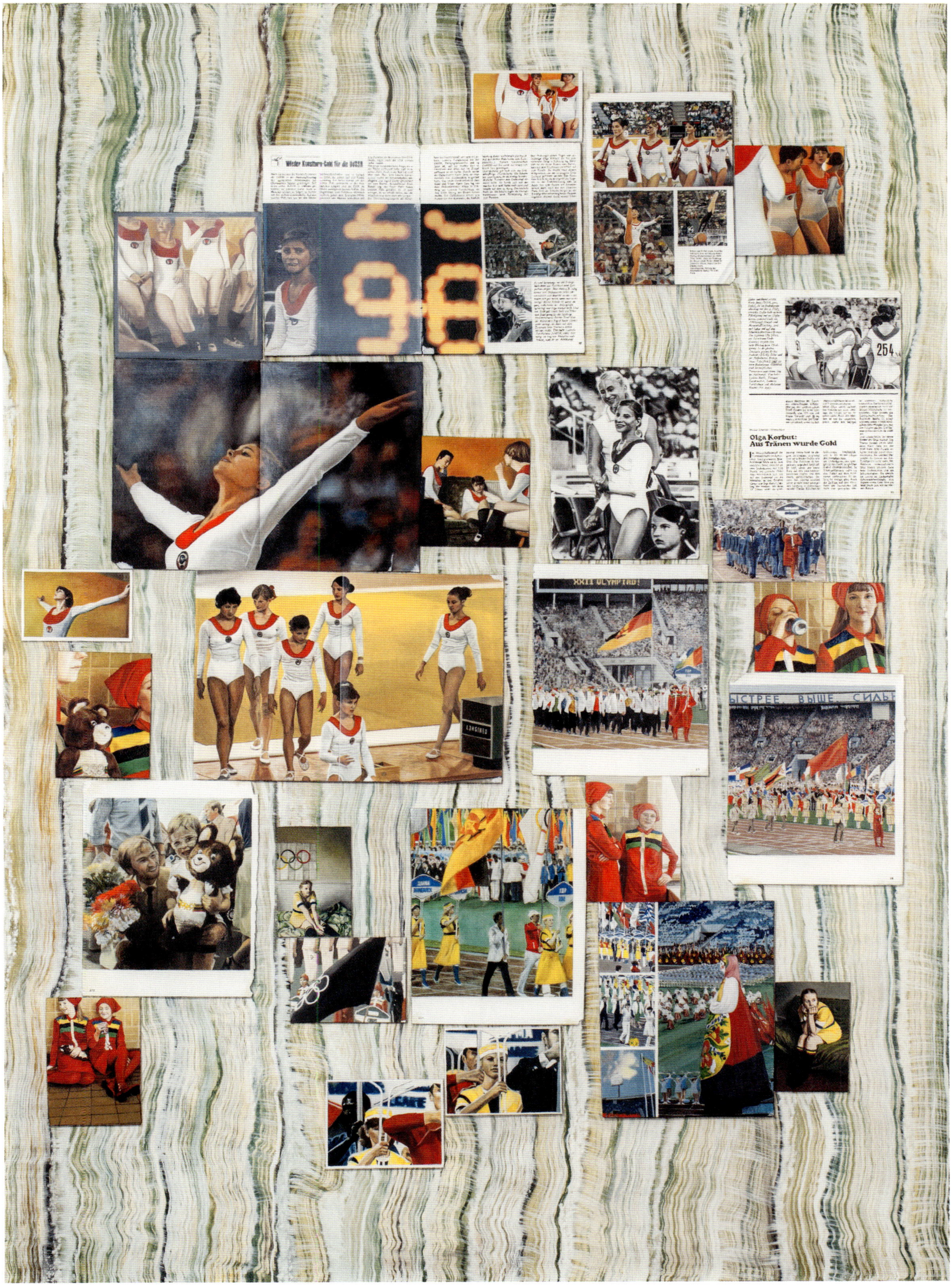

35. Lucy McKenzie, *Quodlibet XXXIV*, 2014

MAIREAD O'HEOCHA

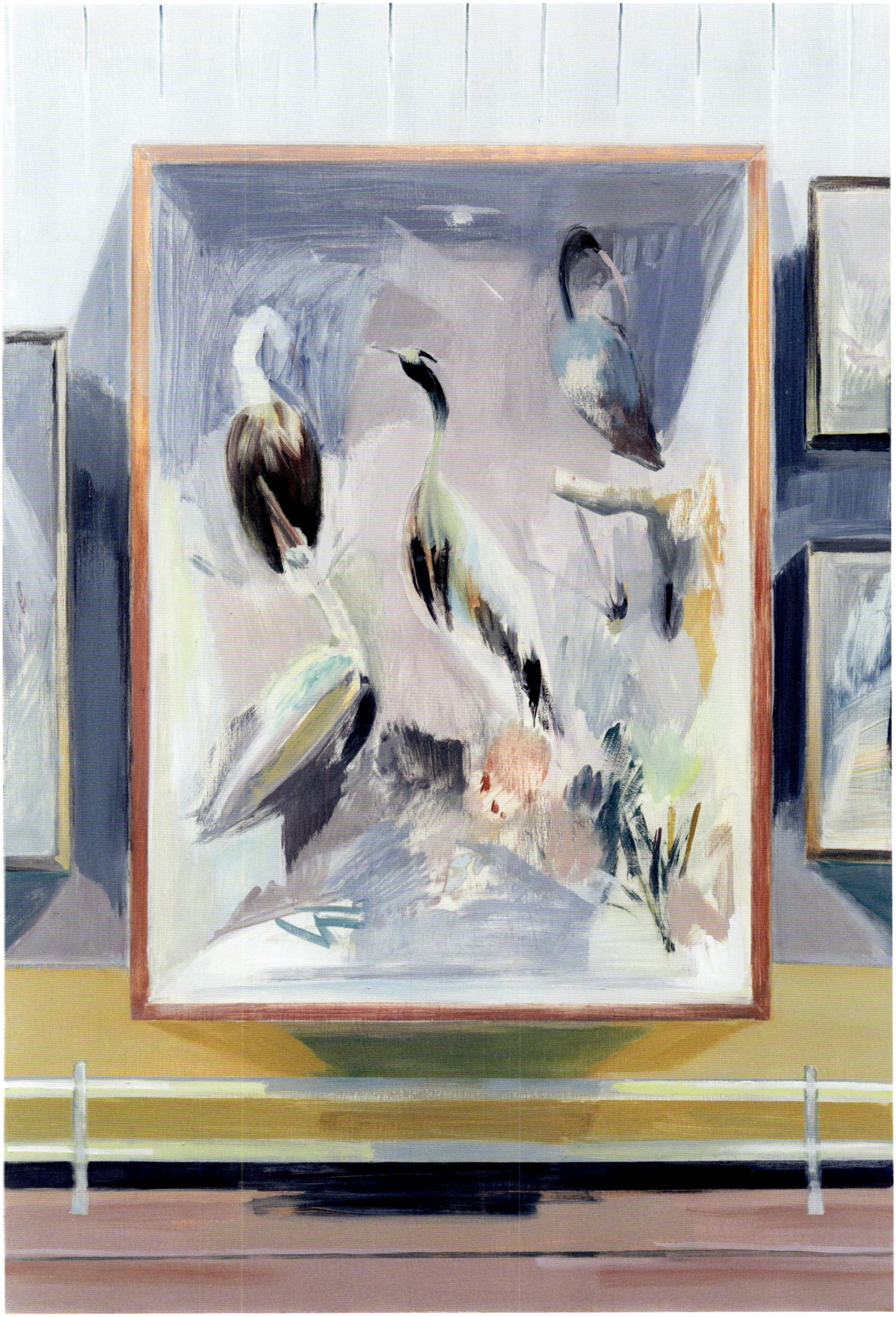

36. Mairead O'hEocha, *Cabinet of Herons, Natural History Museum*, 2018

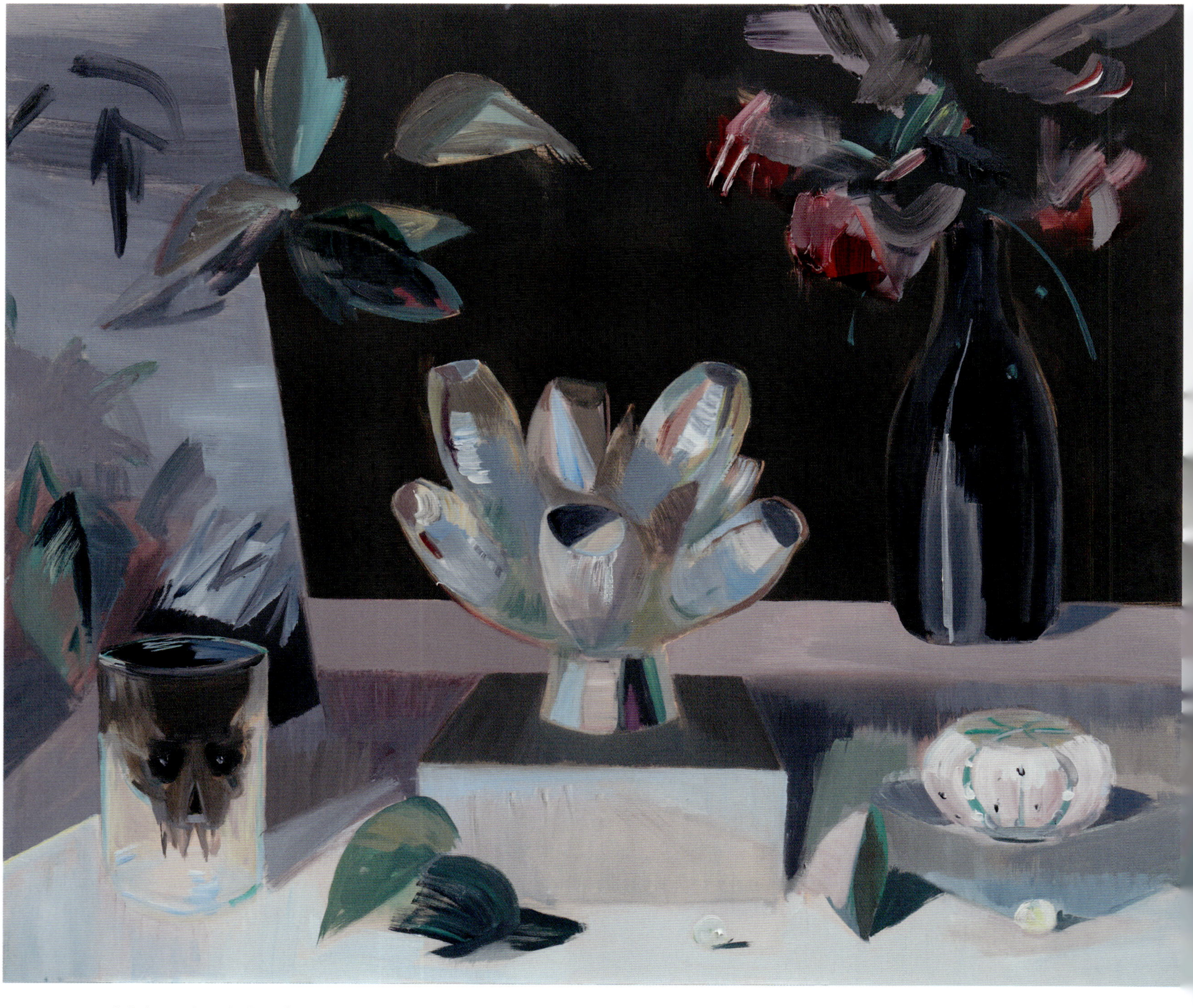

37. Mairead O'hEocha, *Still Life with Skull, Coral and Flowers*, 2018

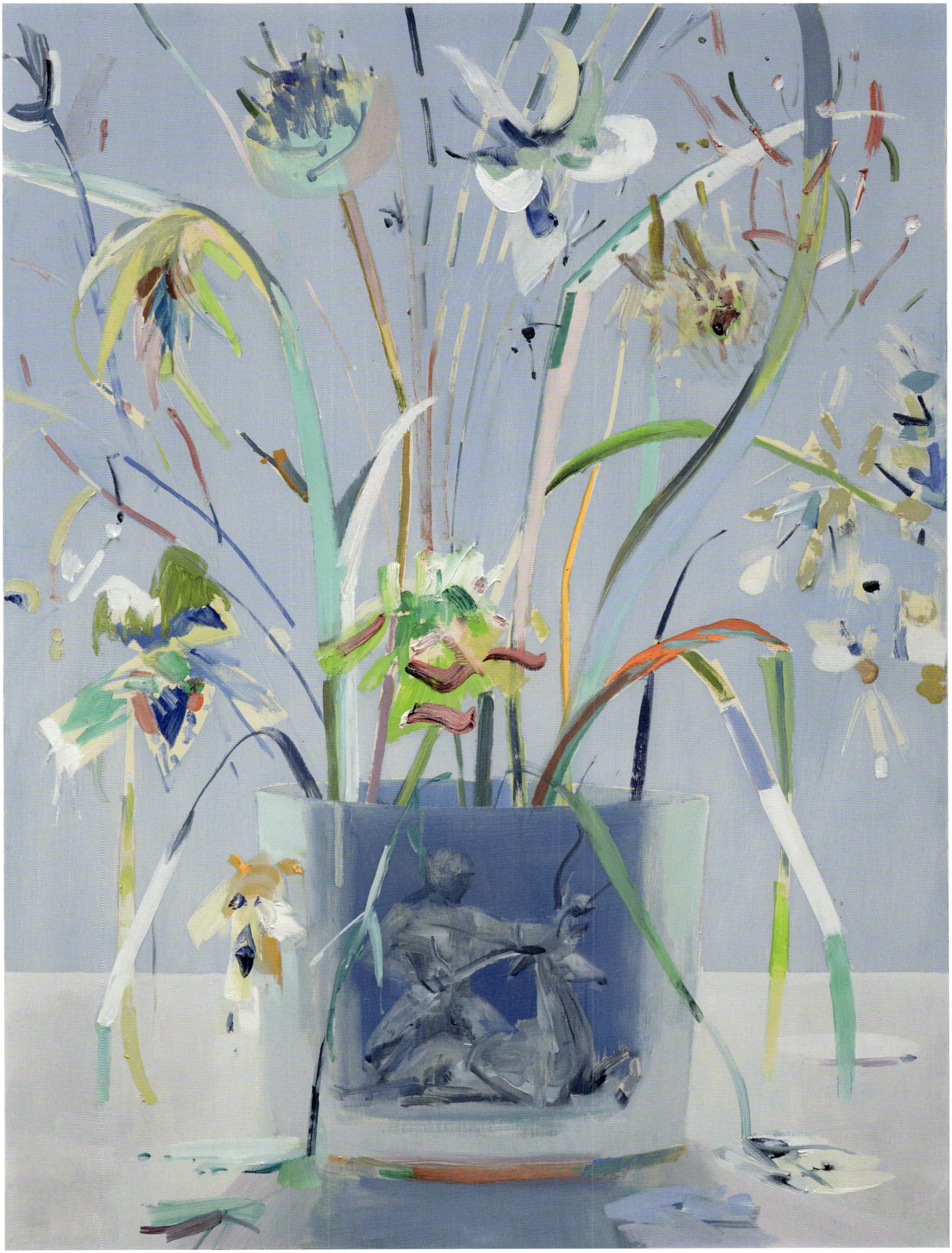

38. Mairead O'hEocha, *Flowers and Herakles*, 2015

YELENA POPOVA

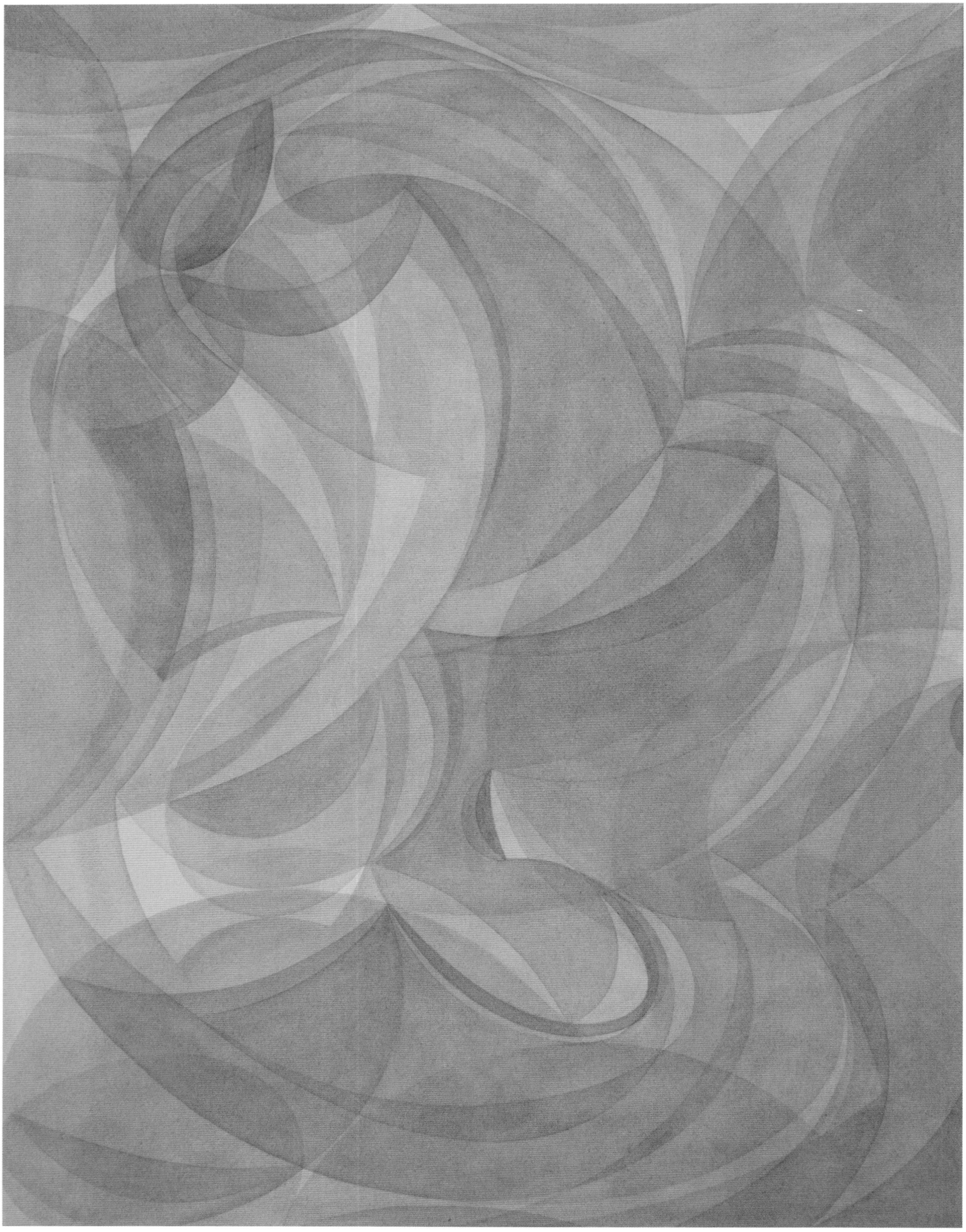

39. Yelena Popova, *Low Parkamoor, 200 Metres above the East Shore of Lake Coniston, Cumbria*, 2018–19

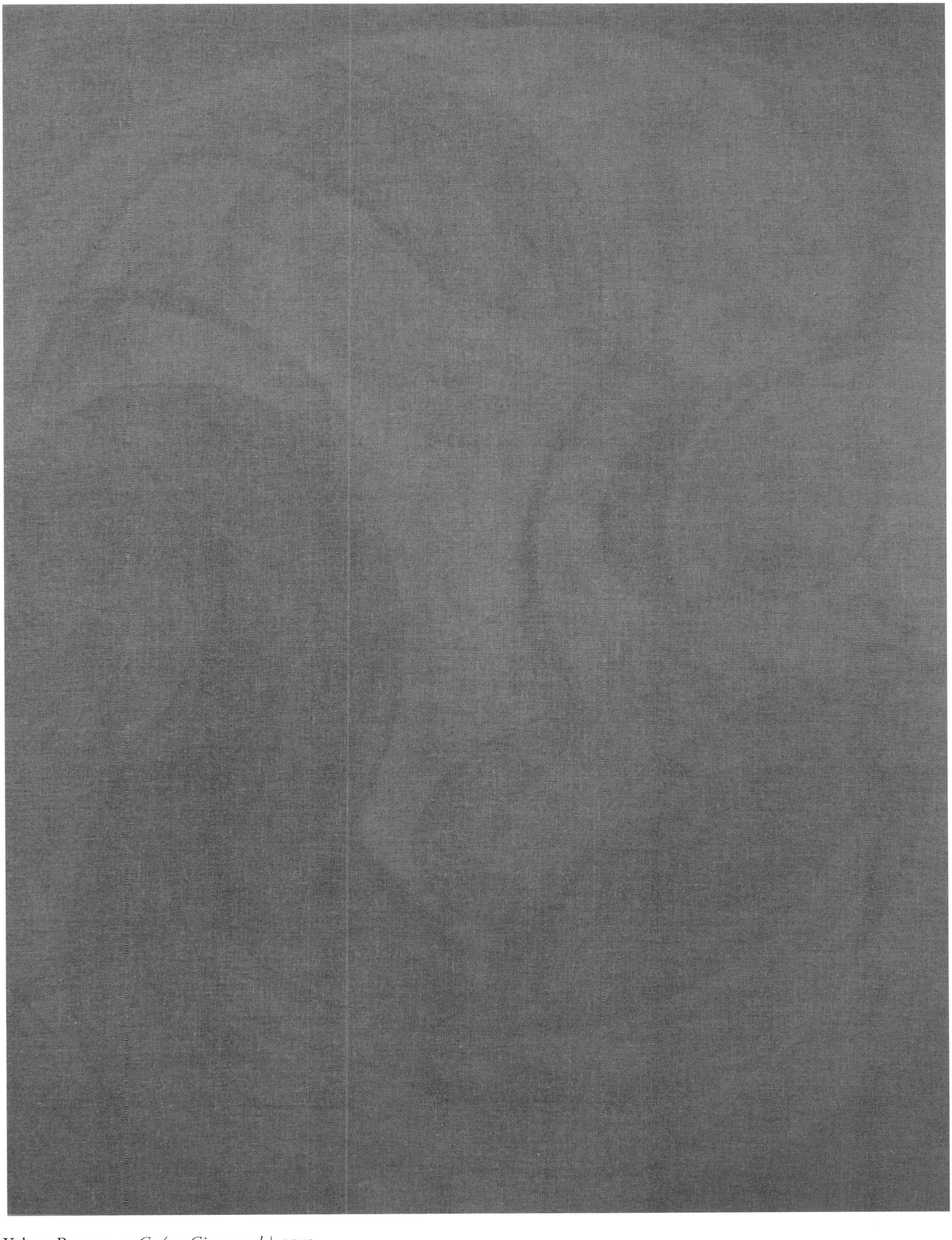

40. Yelena Popova, *2.5Gs (2.5 Gigaseconds)*, 2019

CAROL RHODES

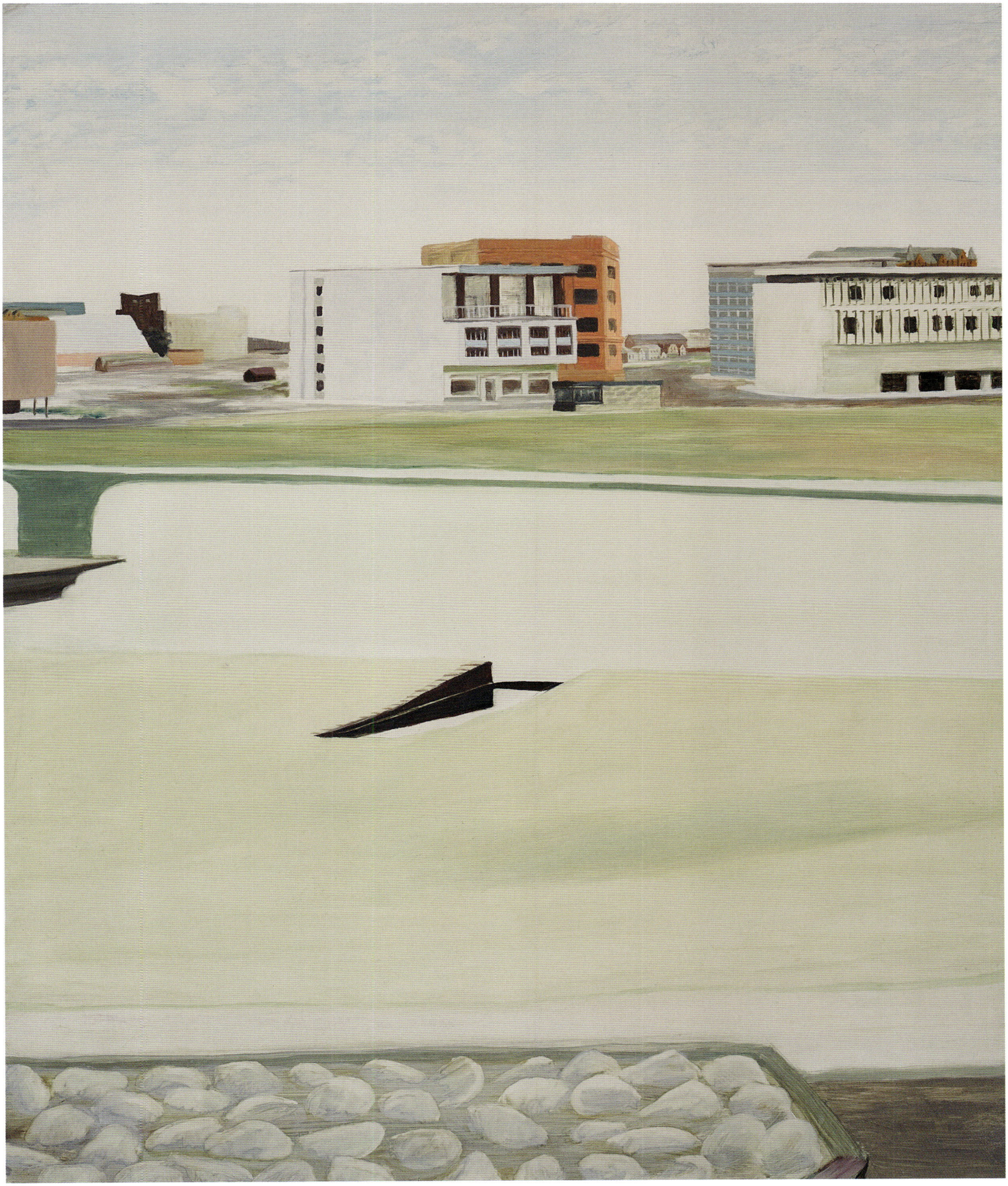

41. Carol Rhodes, *Buildings*, 1994

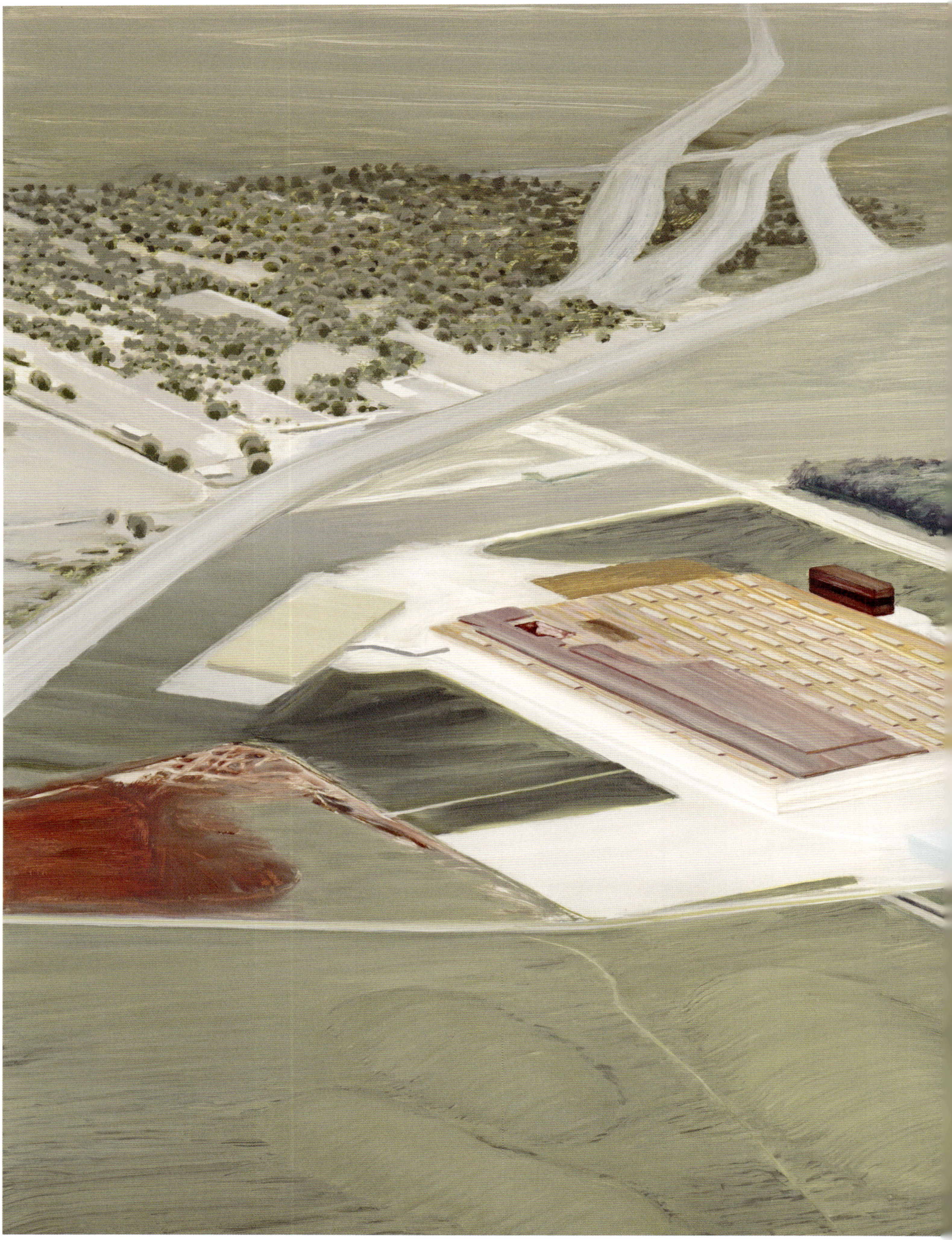

42. Carol Rhodes, *Factory Roof, Countryside*, 2002

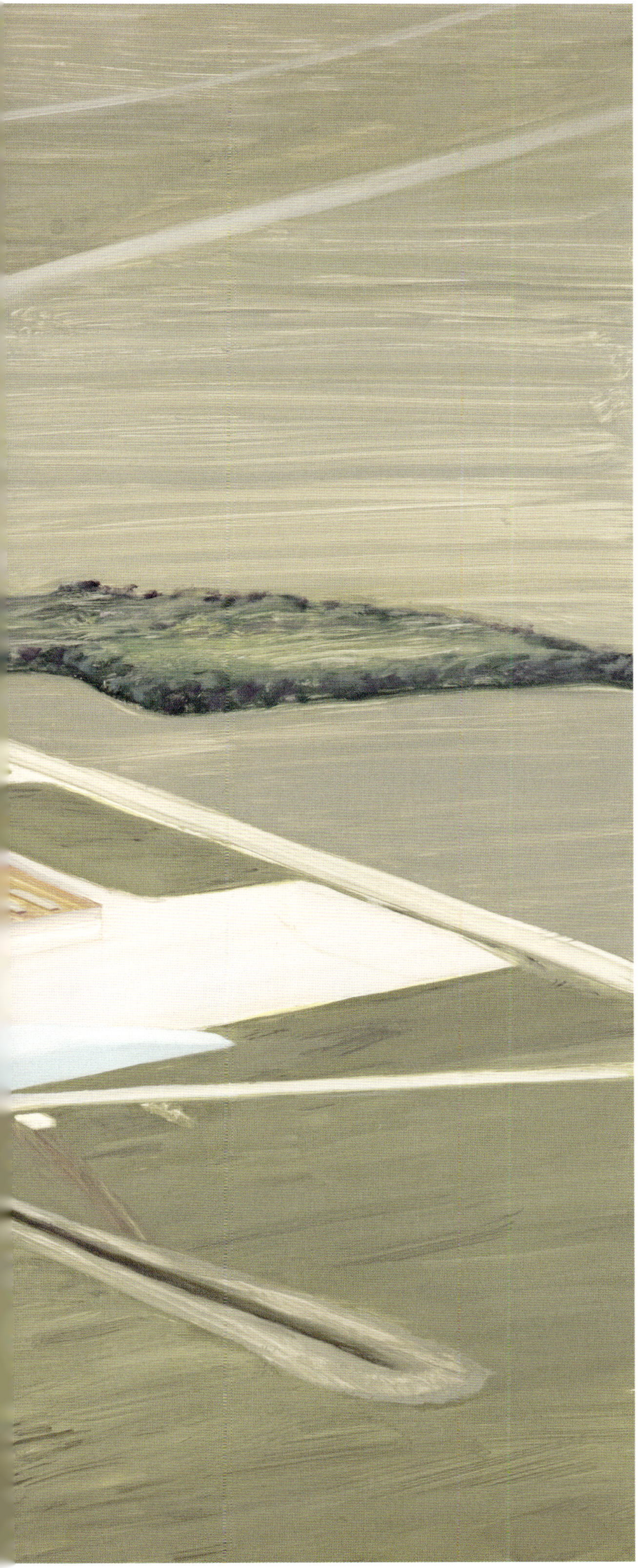

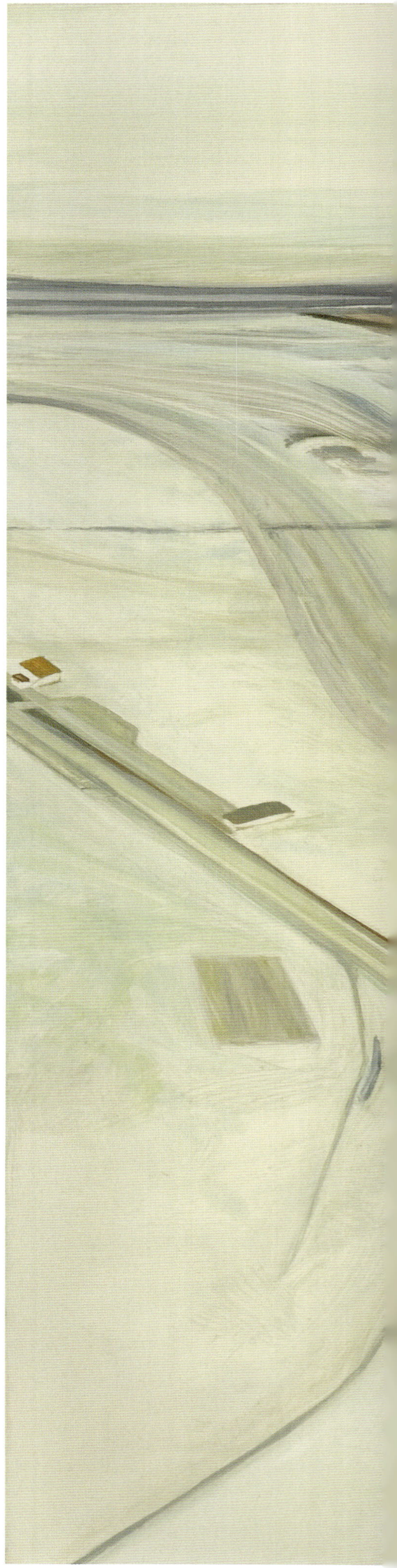

43. Carol Rhodes, *Industrial Landscape*, 1997

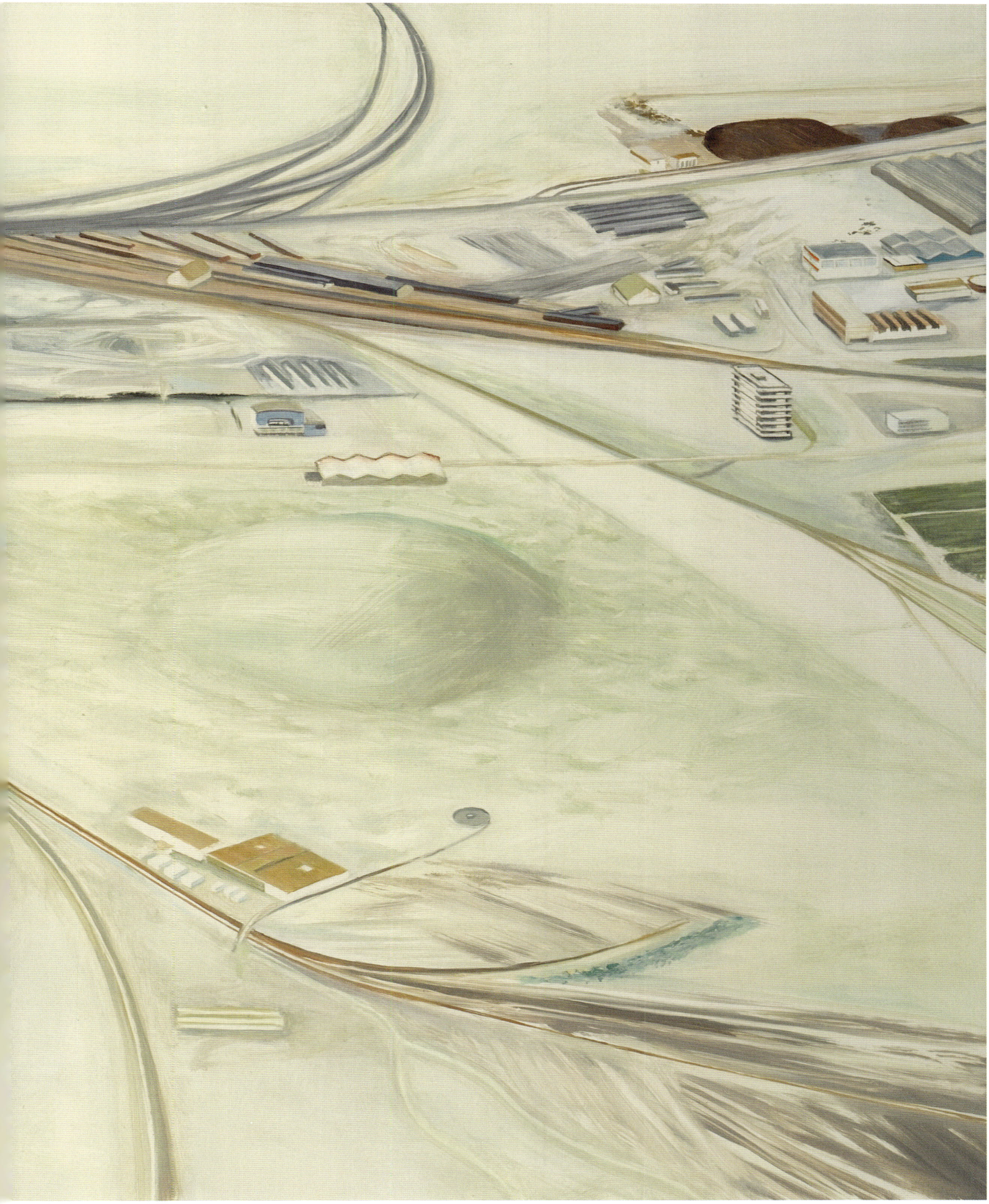

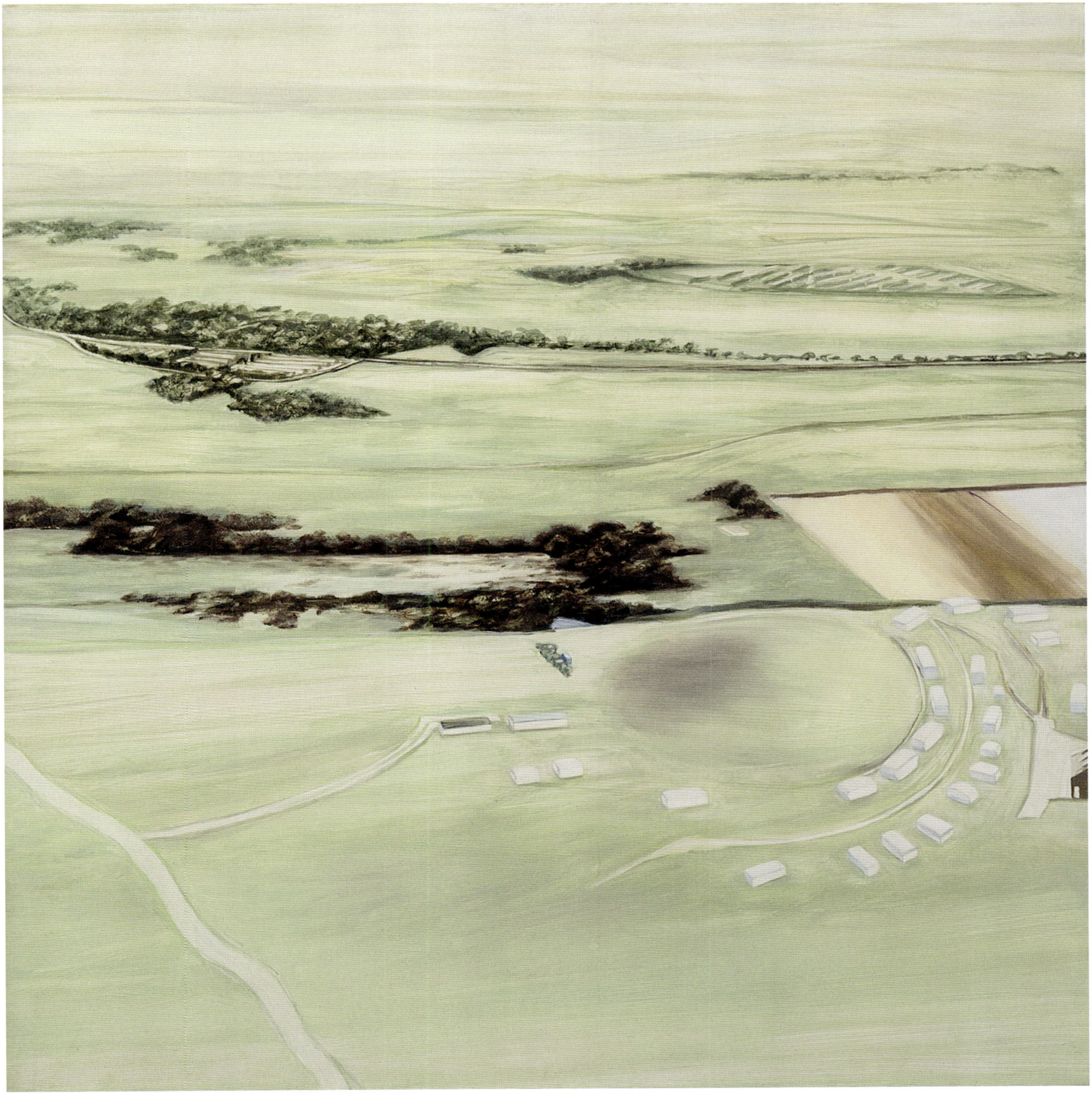

44. Carol Rhodes, *Caravans, View*, 1995–97

SHERMAN MERN TAT SAM

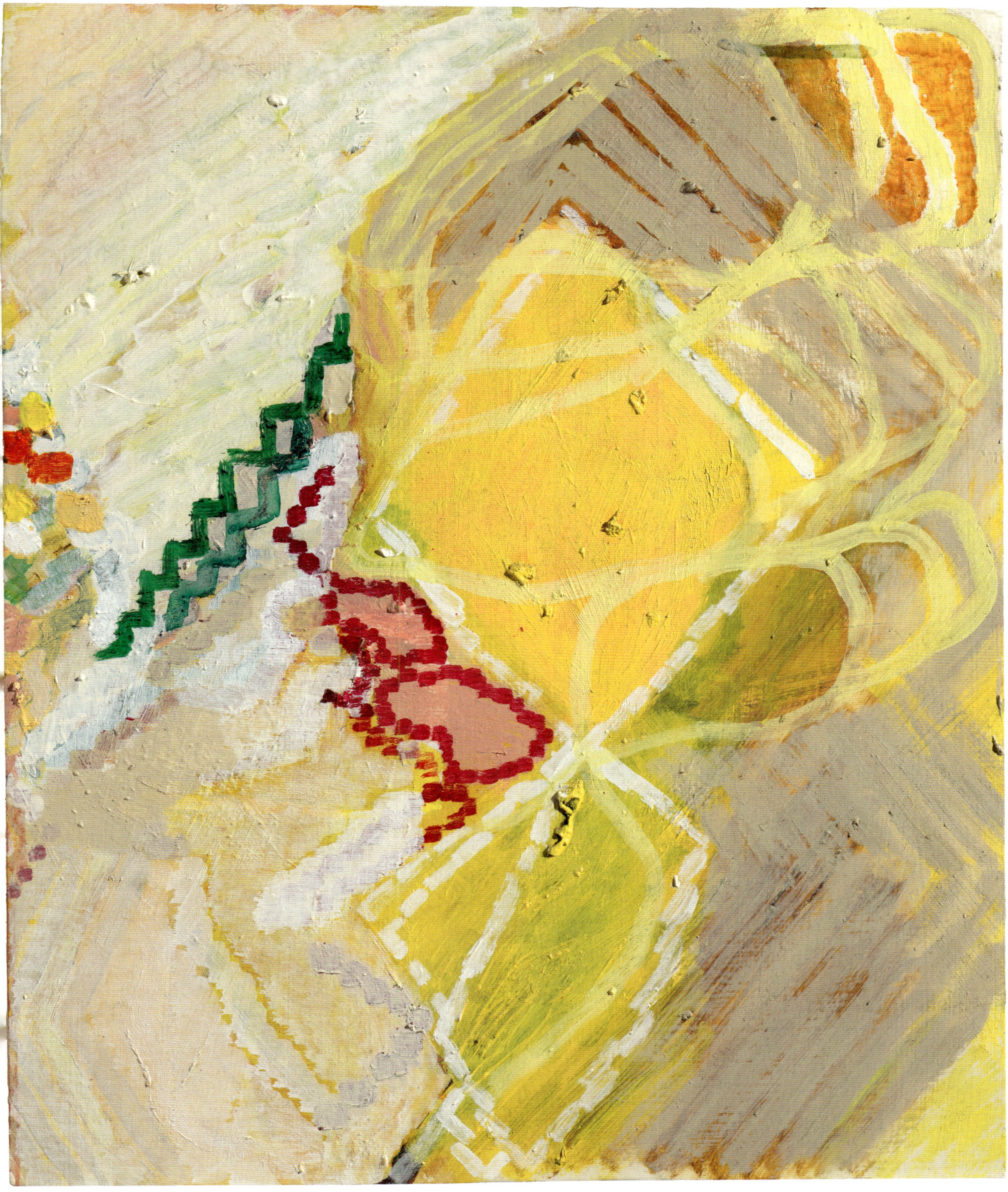

45. Sherman Mern Tat Sam, *Disco Heaven*, 2015

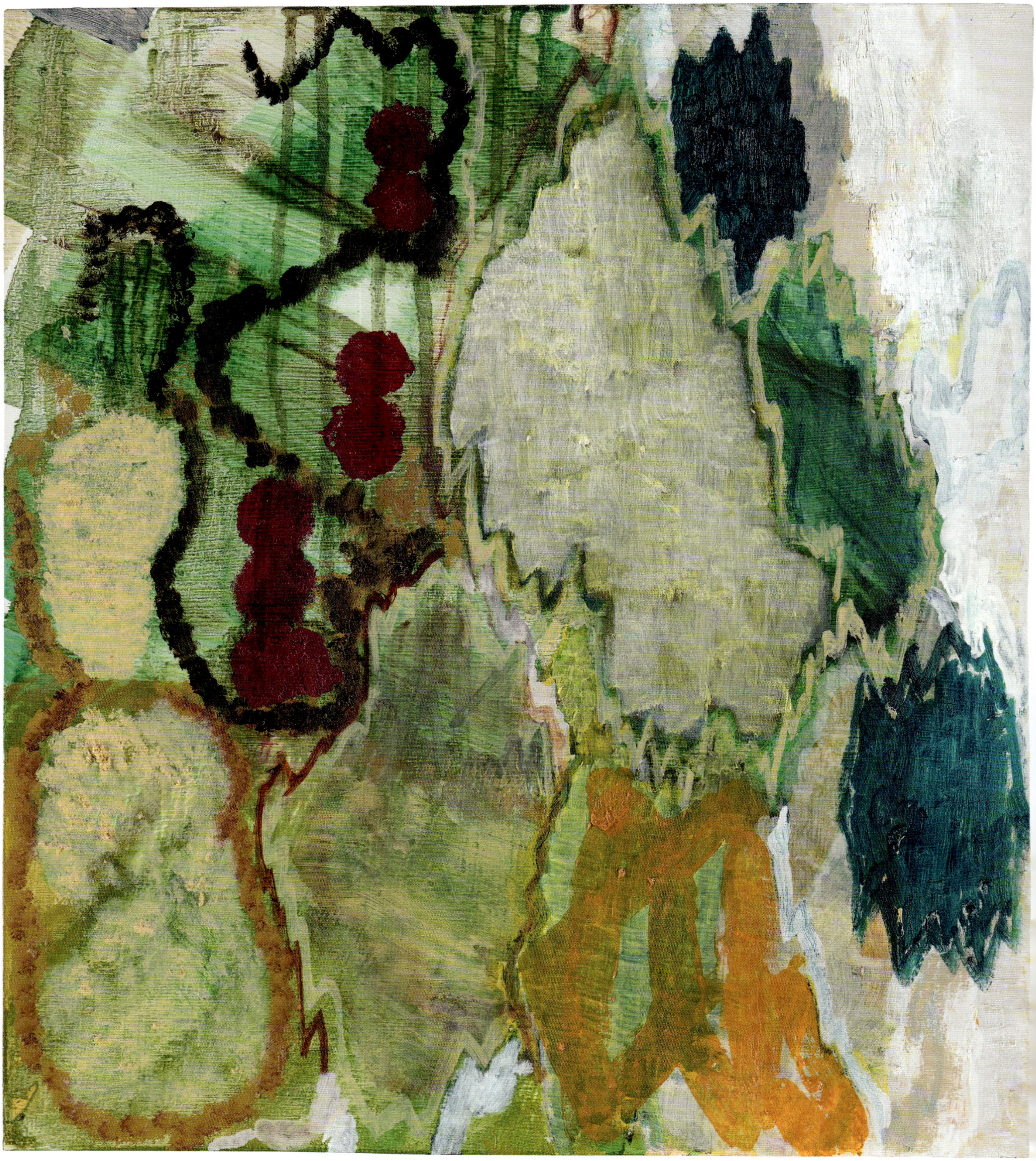

46. Sherman Mern Tat Sam, *Common Ground*, 2014

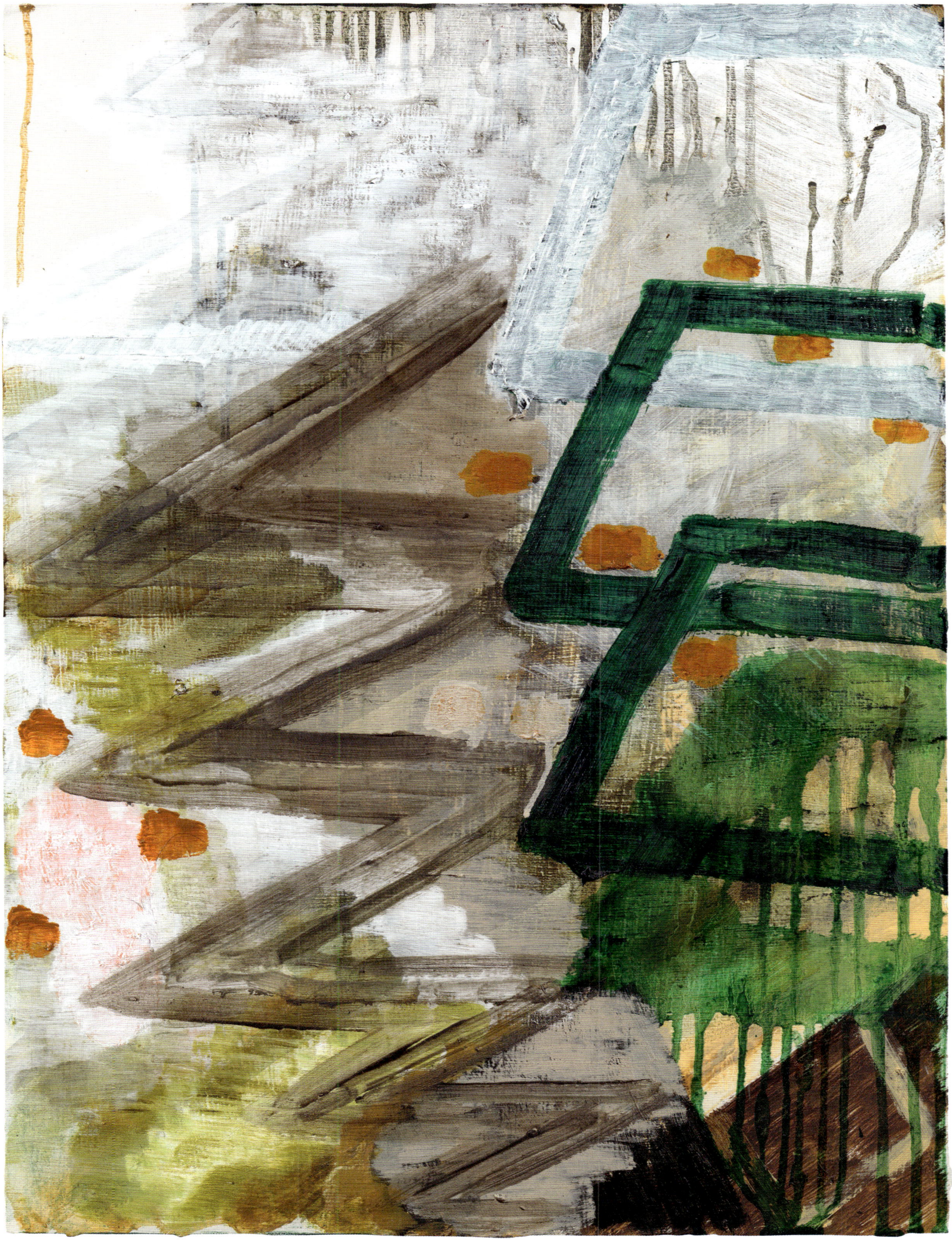

47. Sherman Mern Tat Sam, *Just a Perfect Day*, 2014

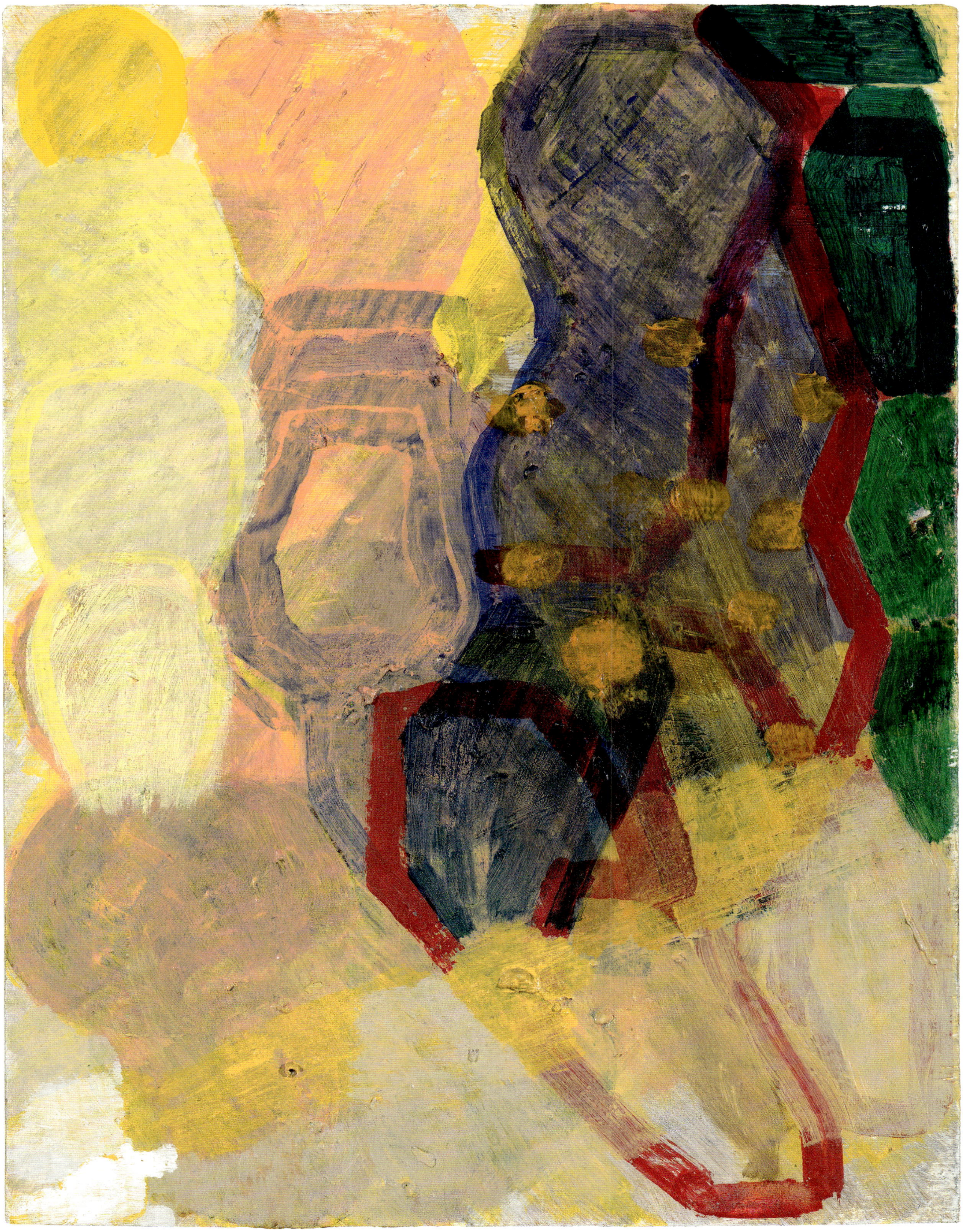

48. Sherman Mern Tat Sam, *Whole Lotta Love*, 2012

BENJAMIN SENIOR

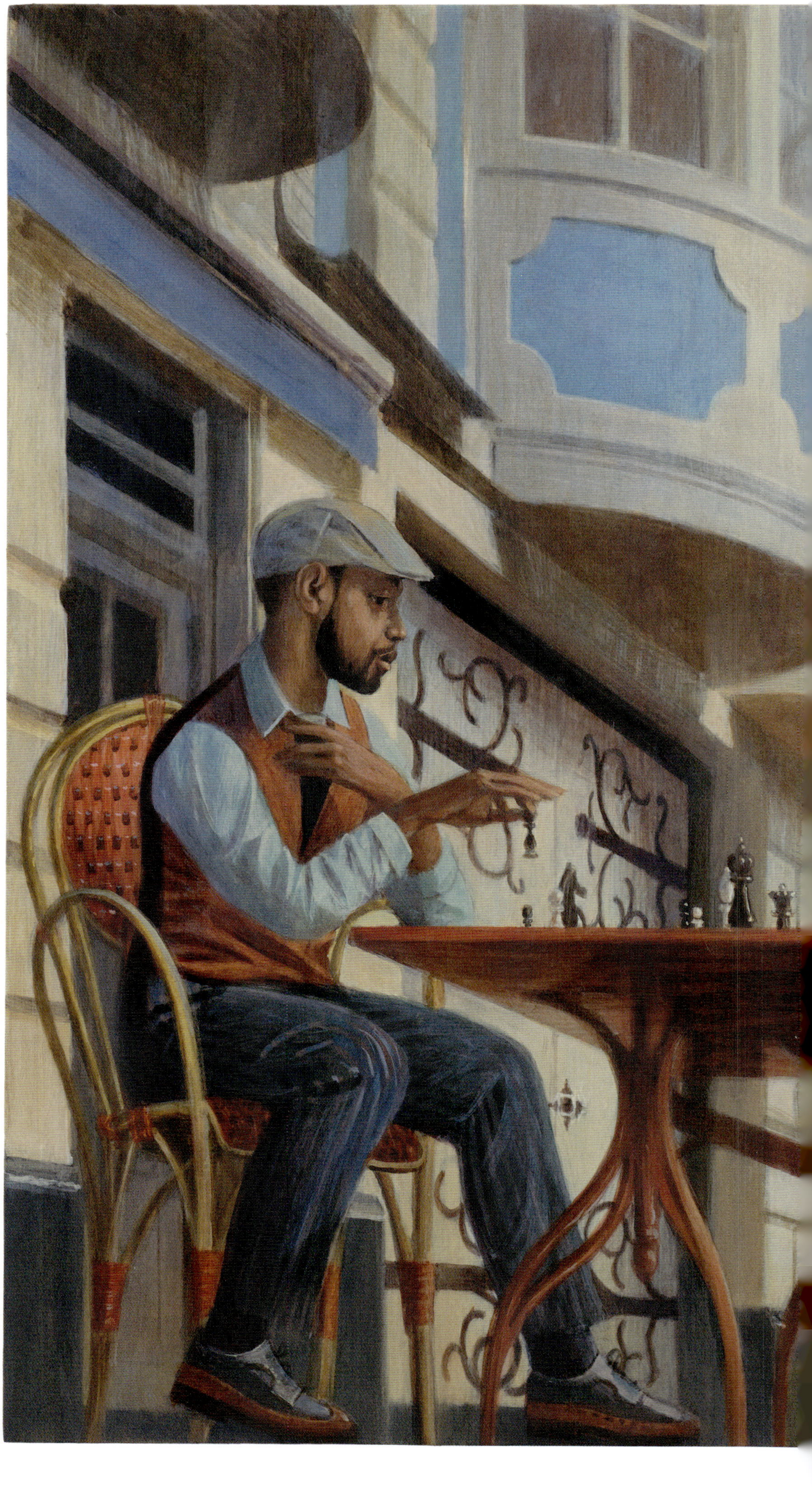

49. Benjamin Senior, *Old Town*, 2019

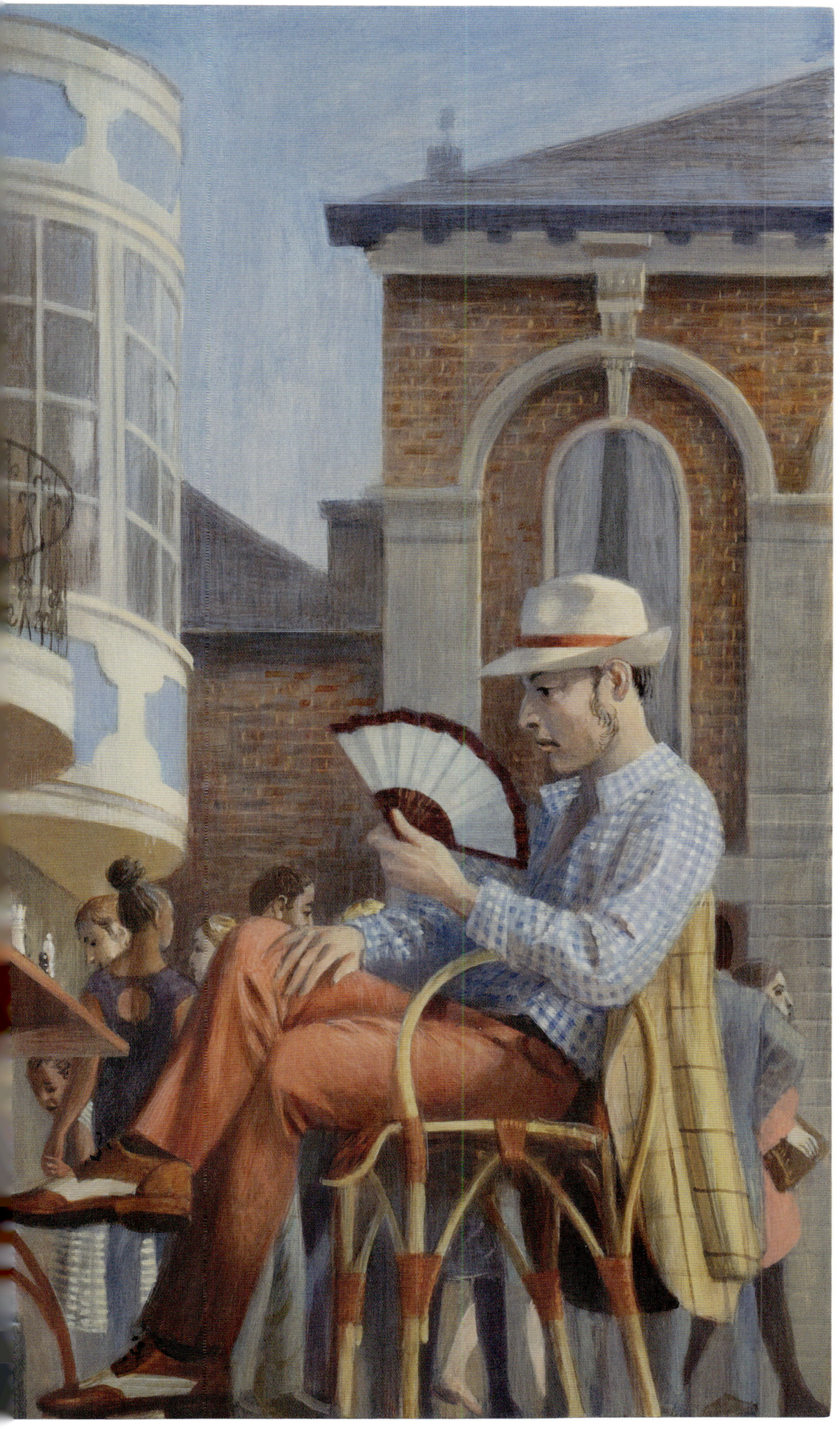

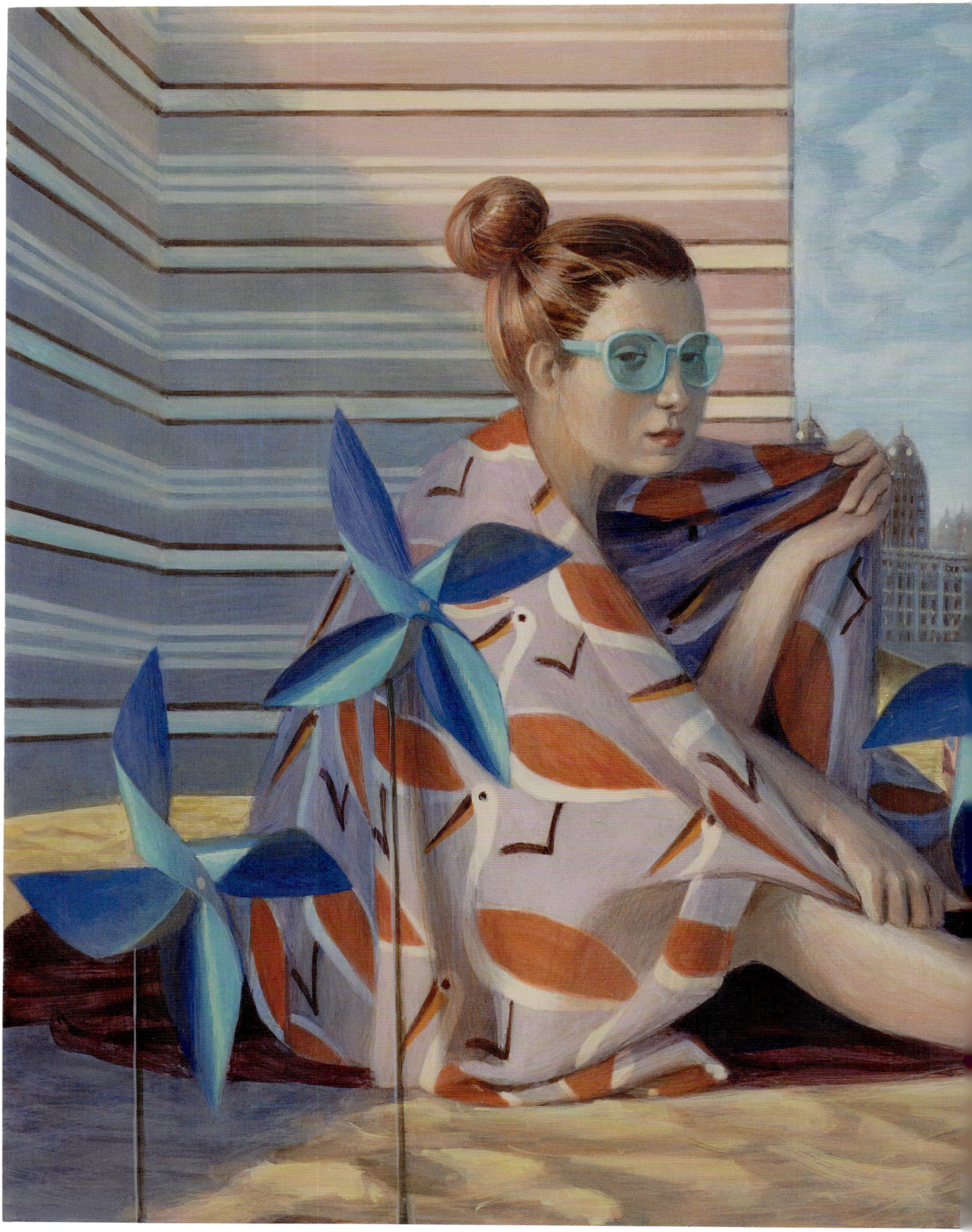

50. Benjamin Senior, *Shade*, 2019

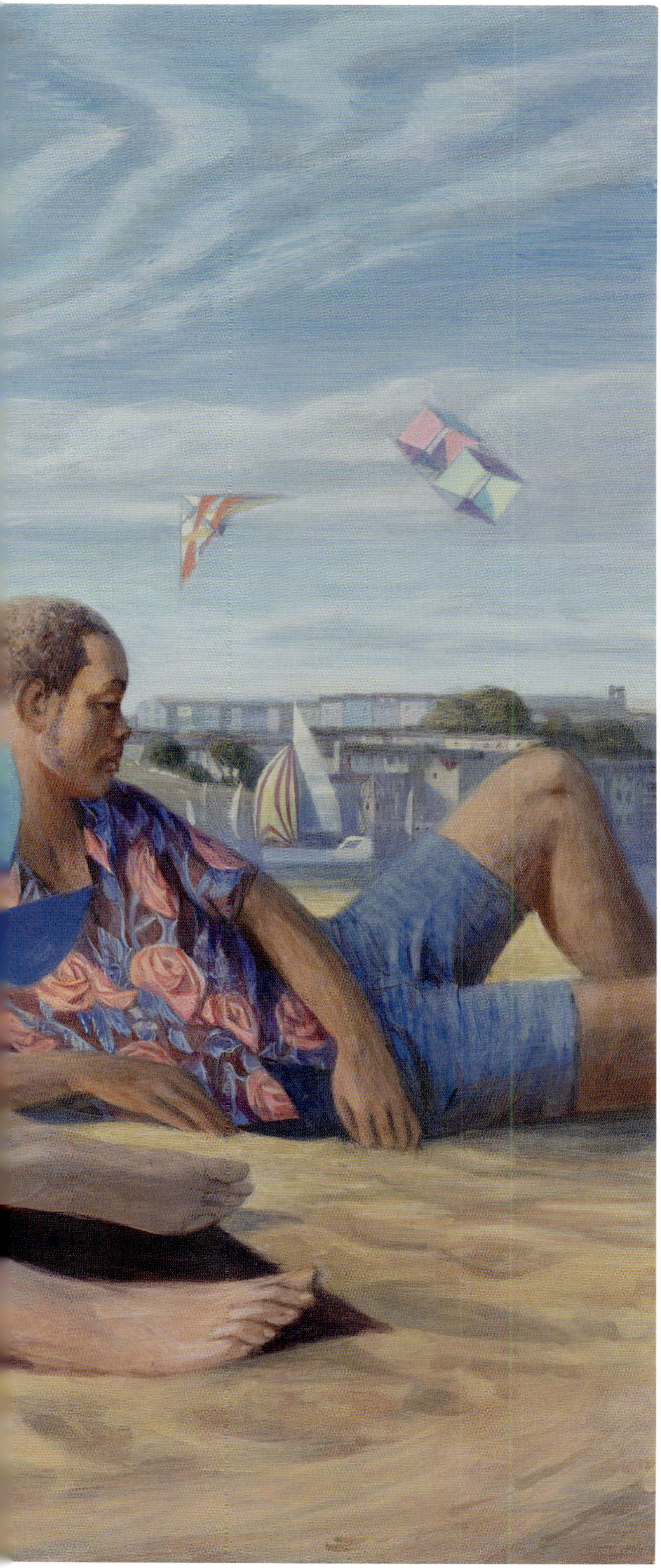

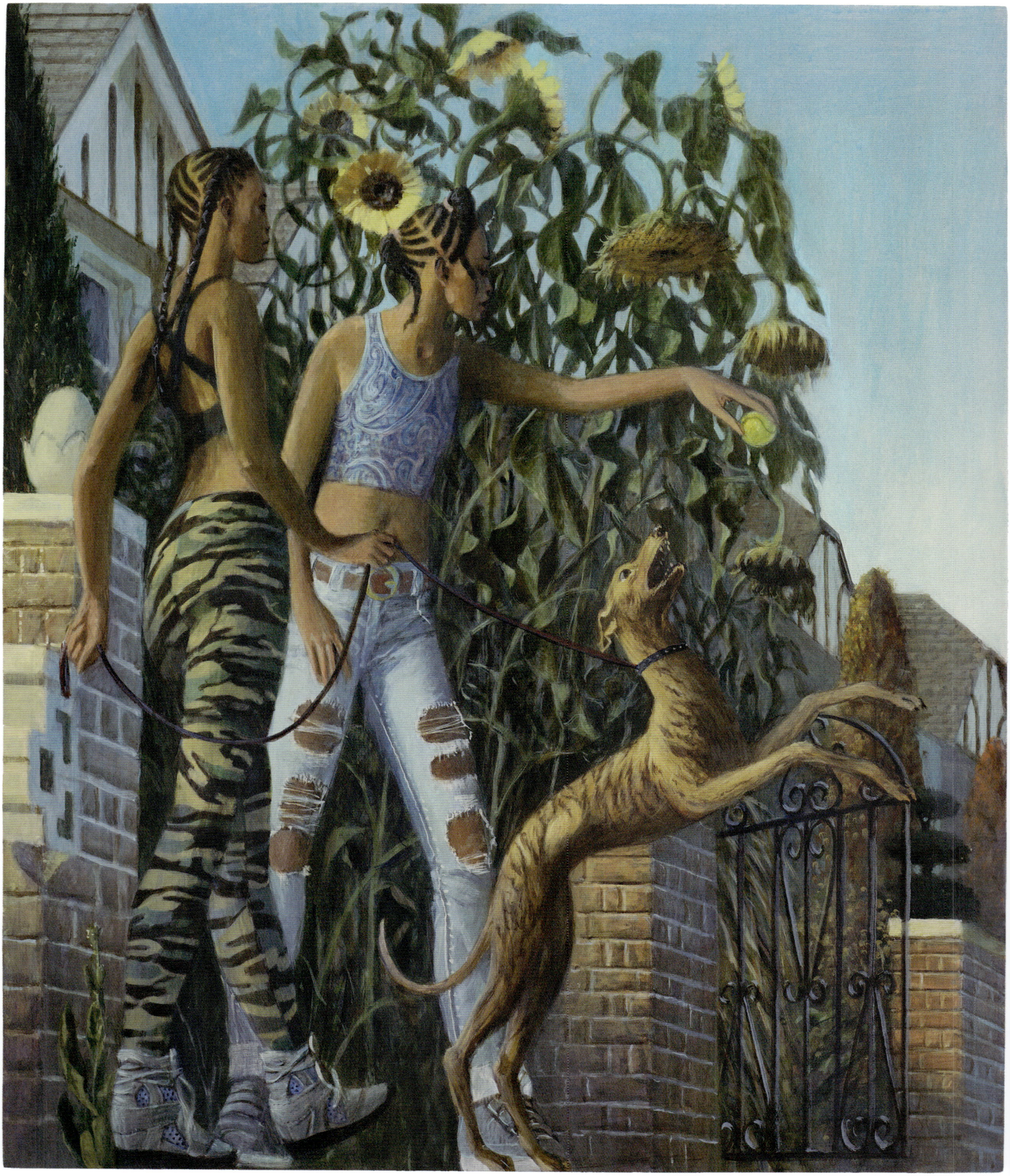

51. Benjamin Senior, *Summersend*, 2018

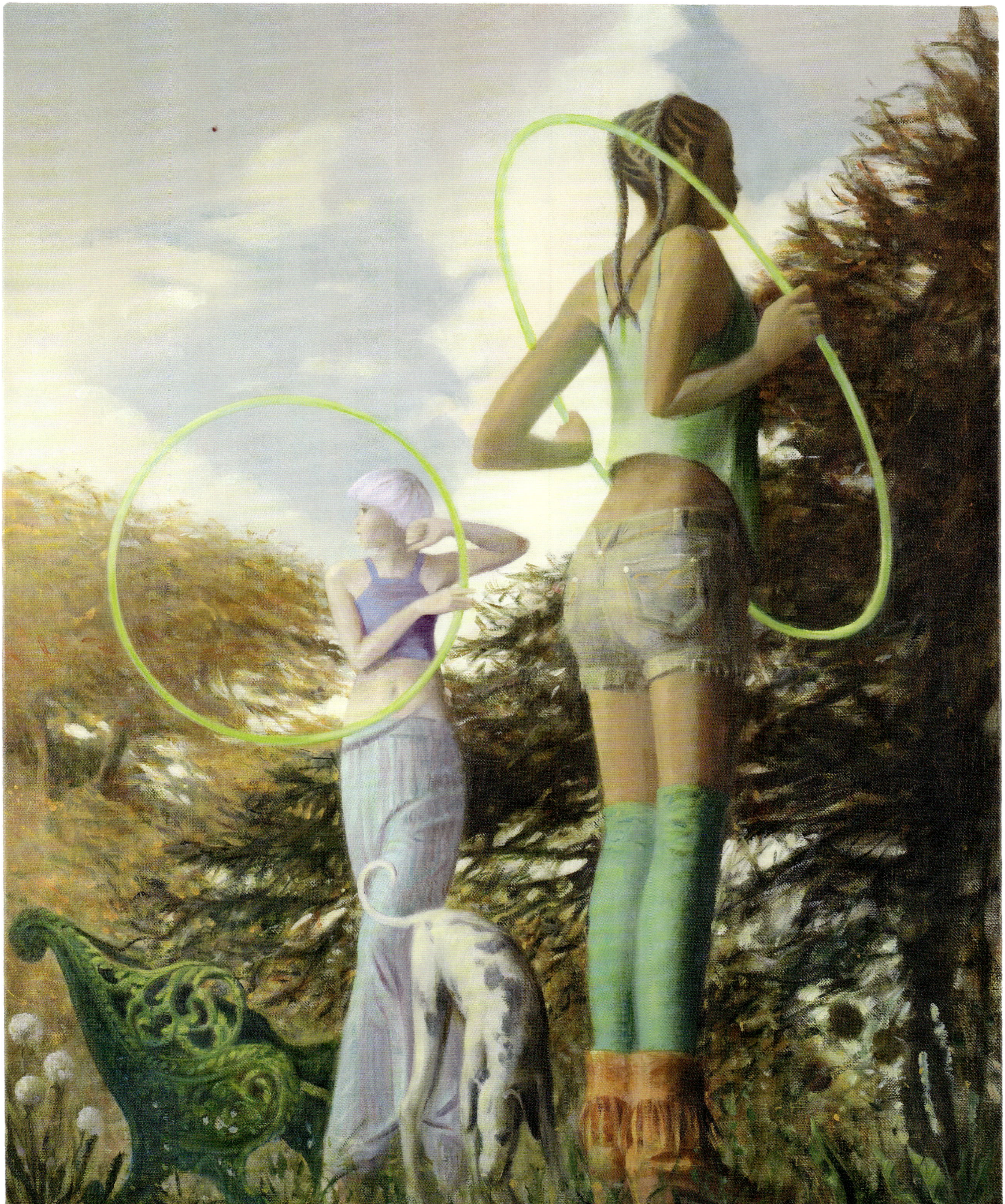

52. Benjamin Senior *Portals*, 2016

MICHAEL SIMPSON

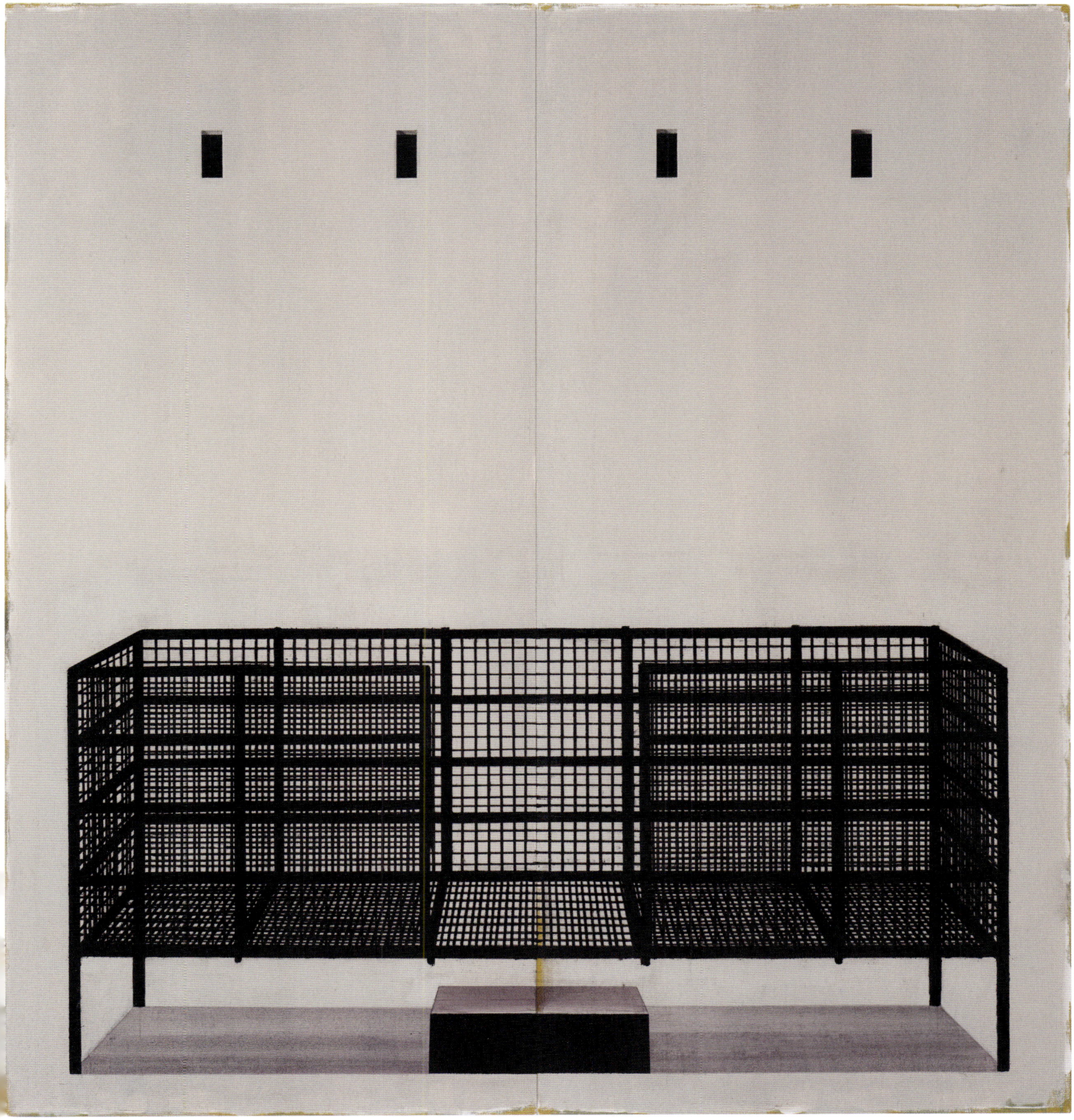

53. Michael Simpson, *Squint 59*, 2017

TIM STONER

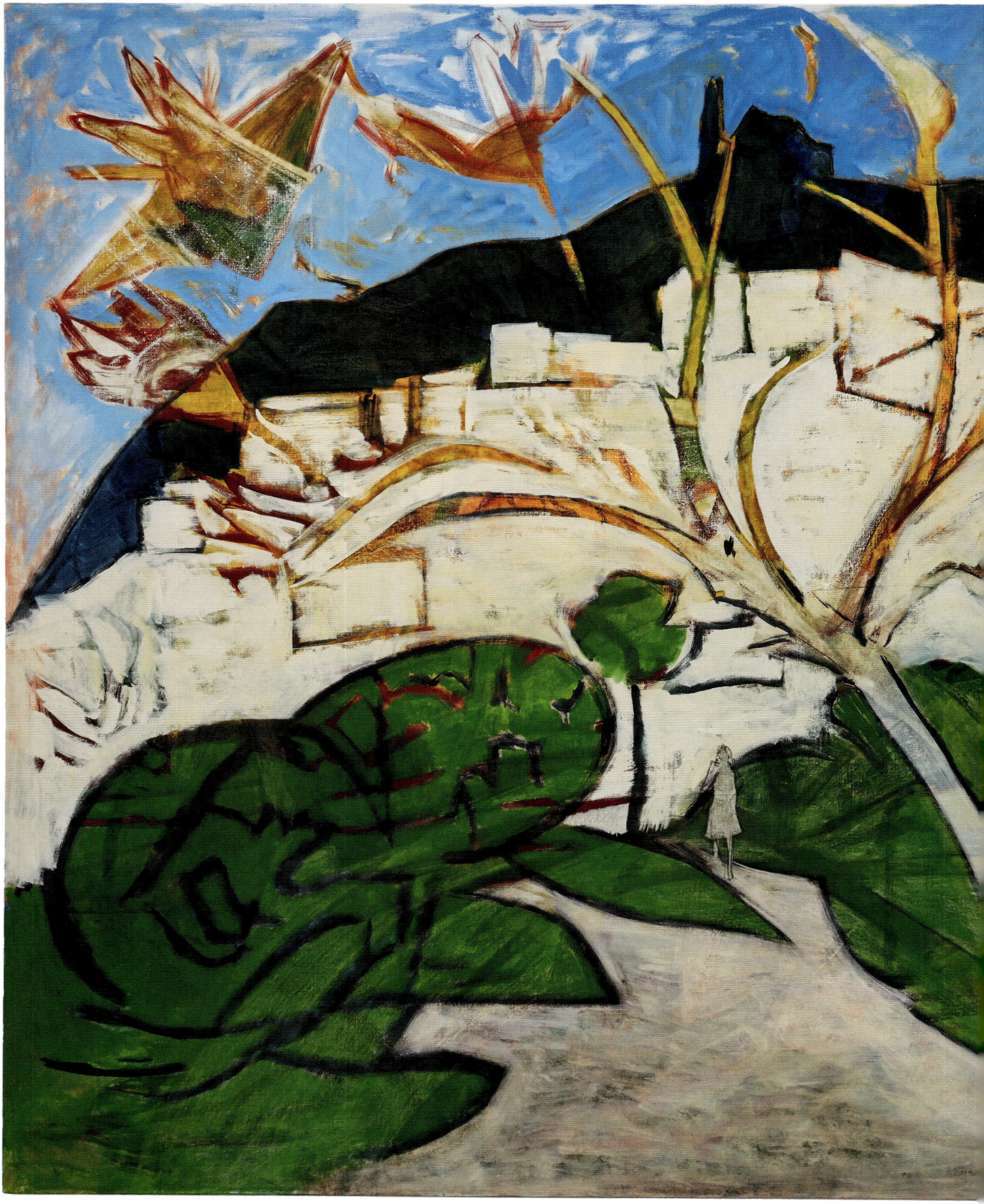

54. Tim Stoner, *Día de los muertos (Casares)*, 2016–19

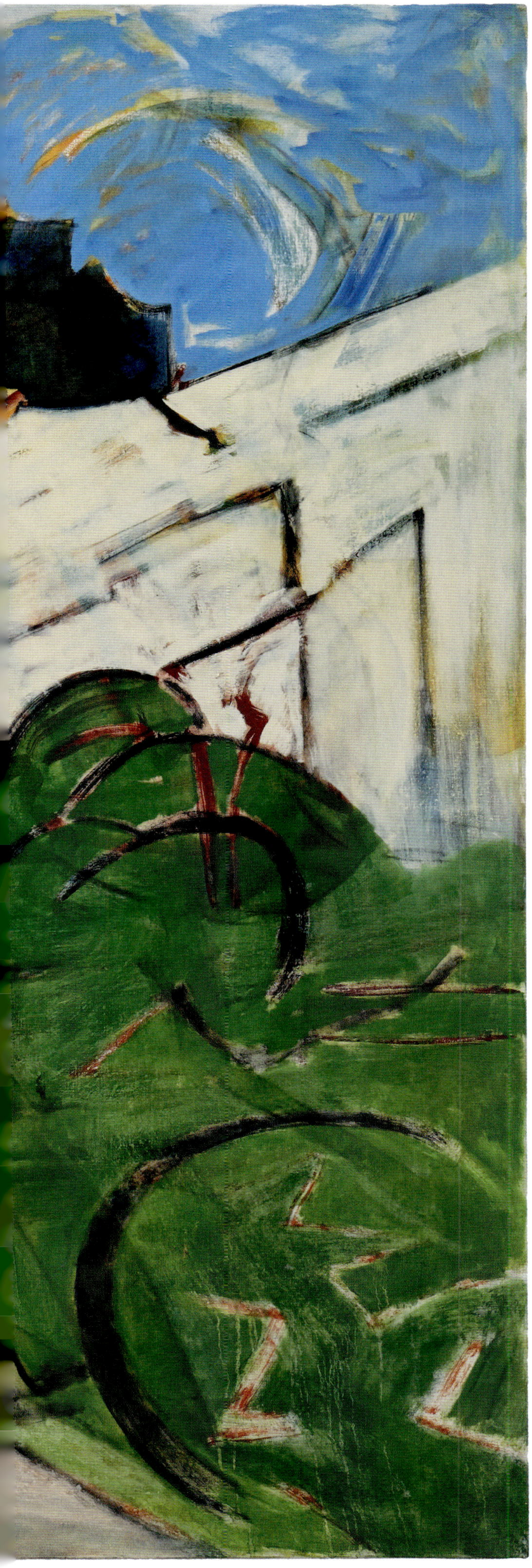

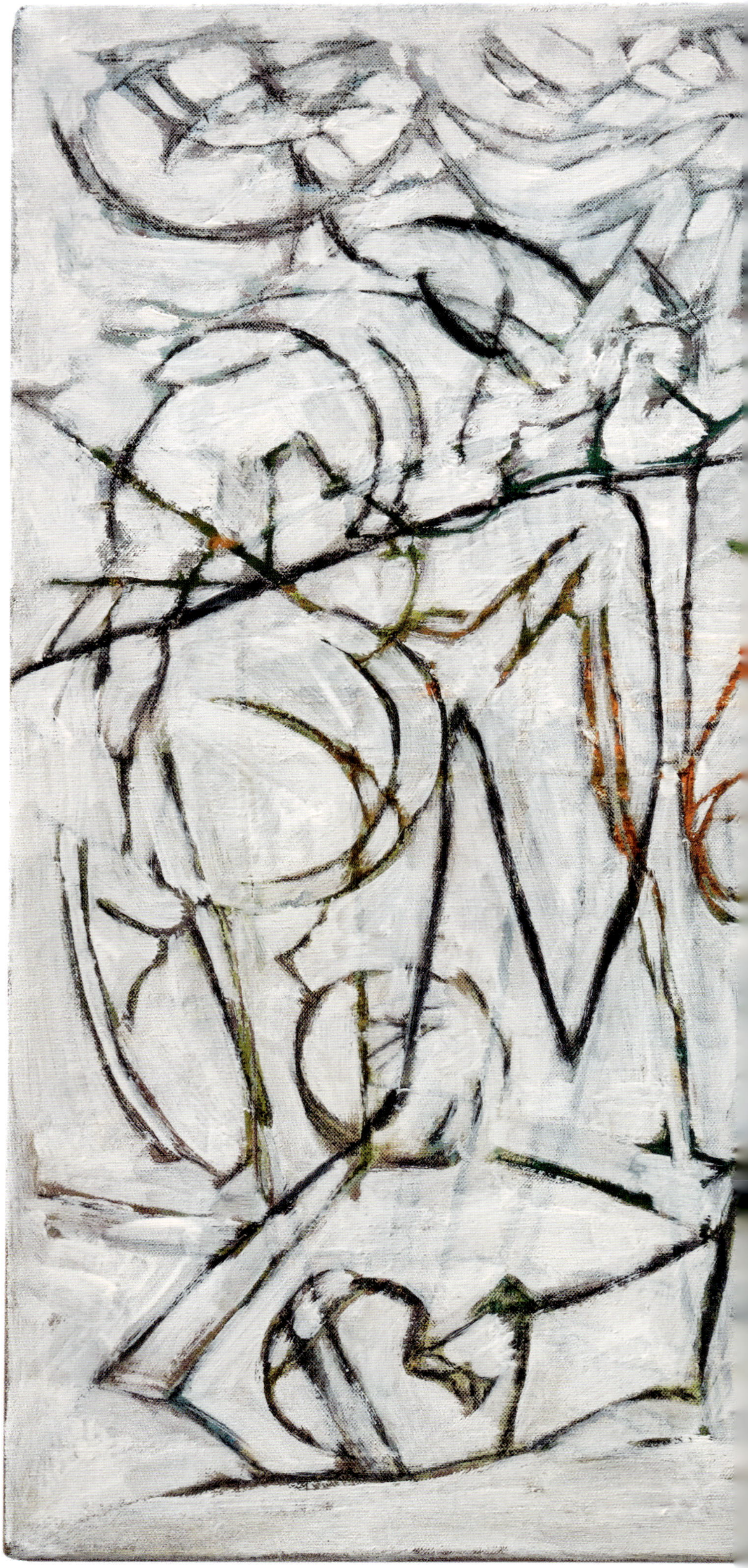

55. Tim Stoner, *Virgen de la Cabeza (Ronda)*, 2019

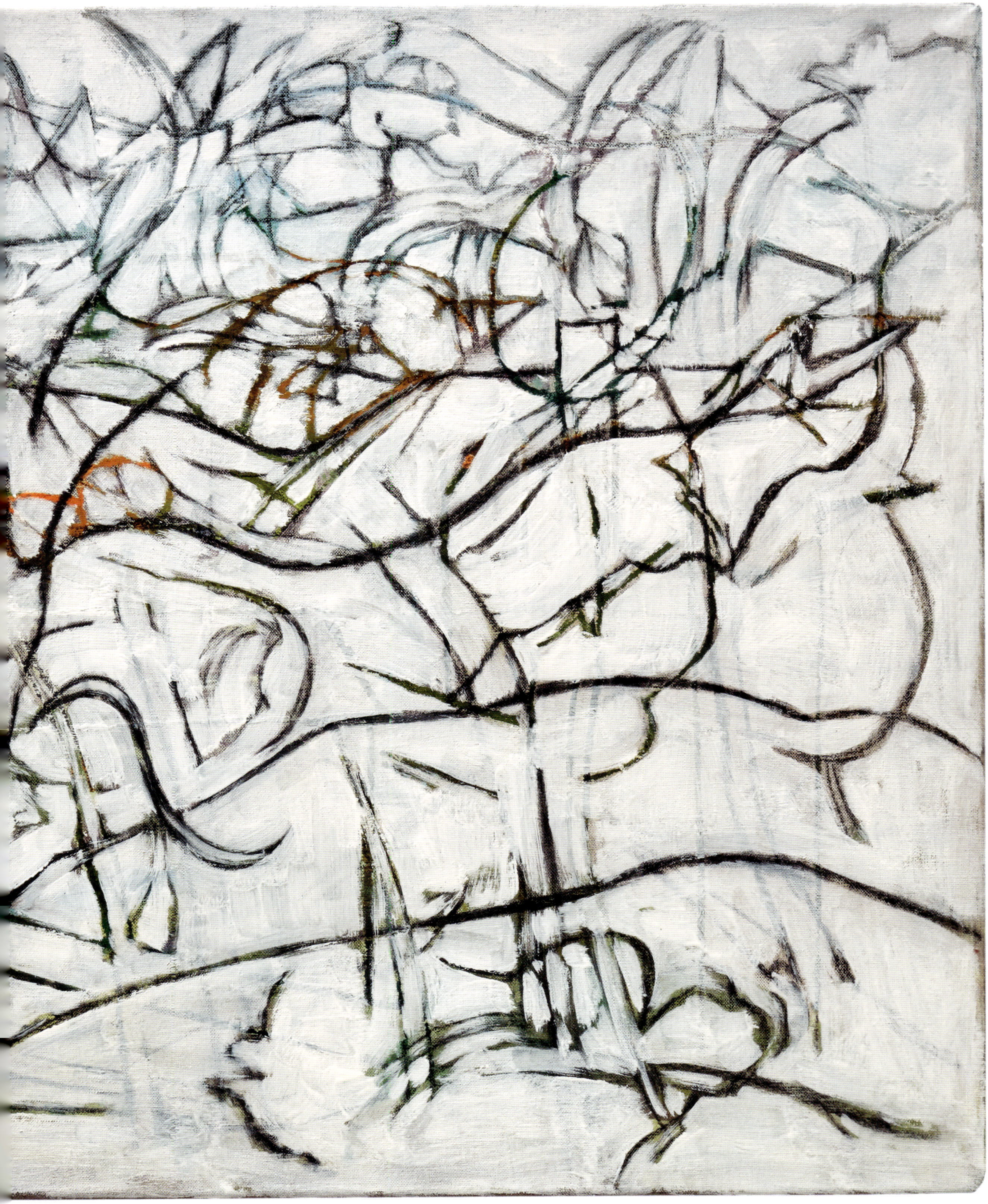

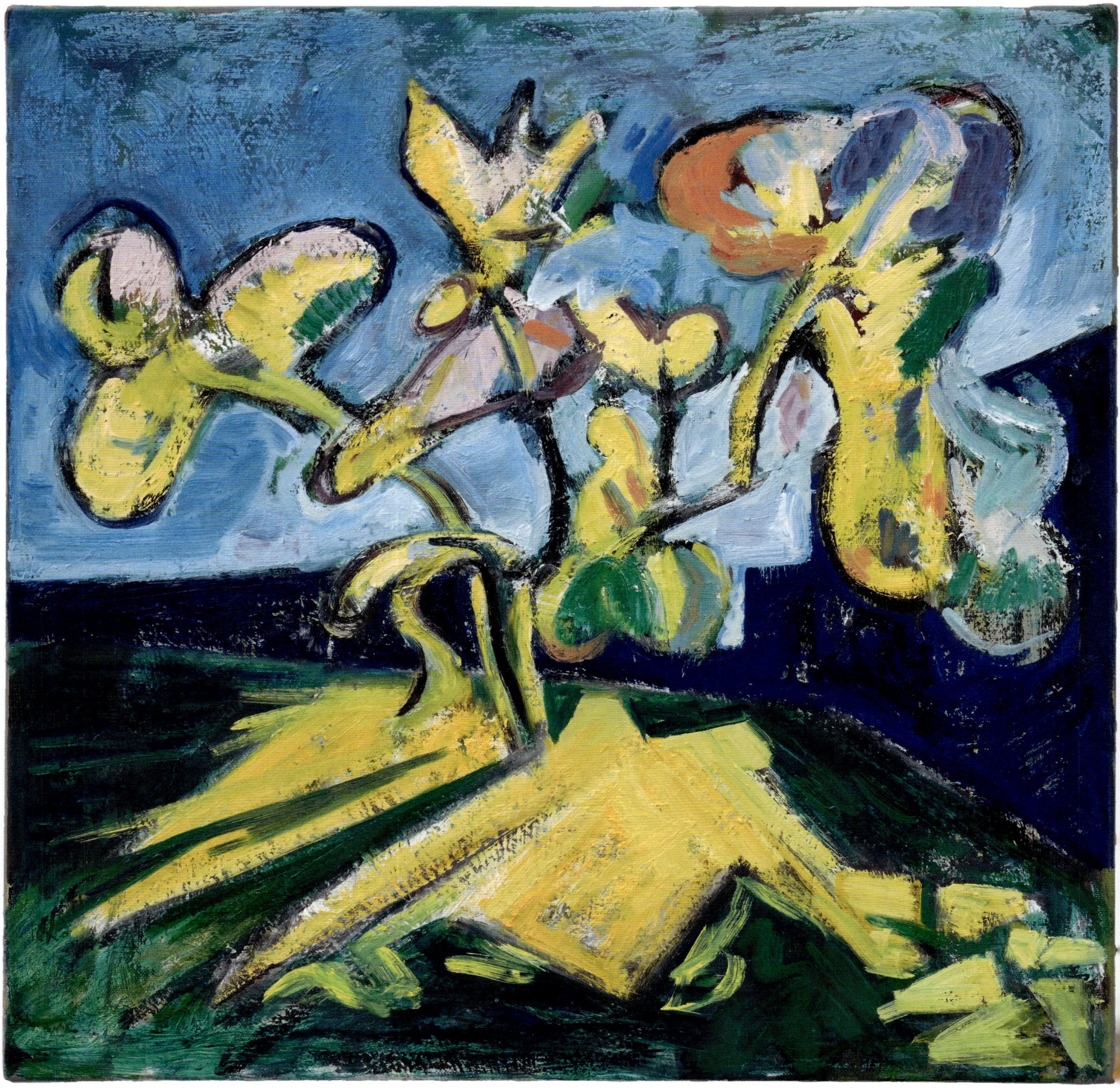

56. Tim Stoner, *Jardín (Ronda)*, 2018

CARAGH THURING

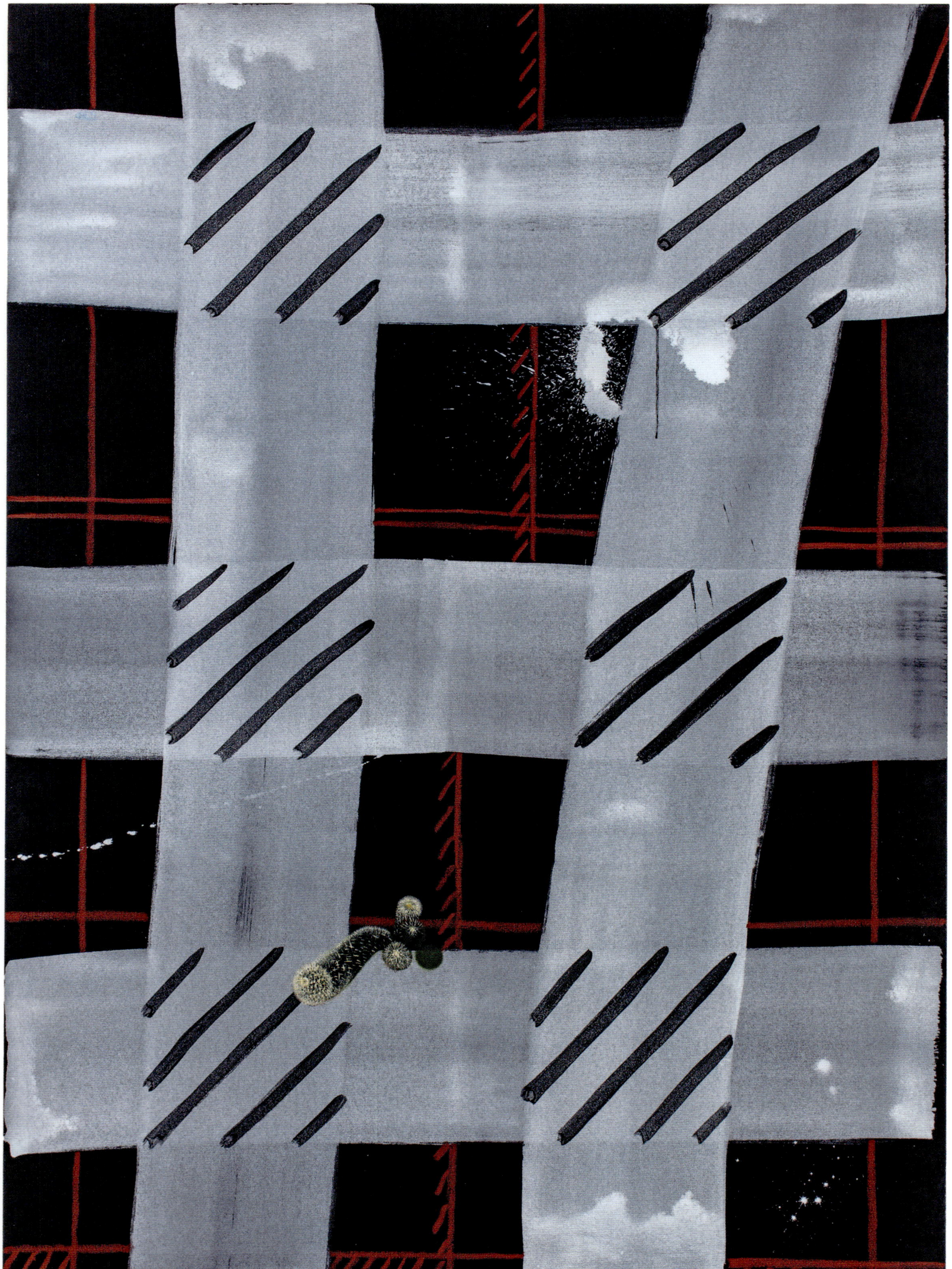

57. Caragh Thuring, *Roger*, 2018

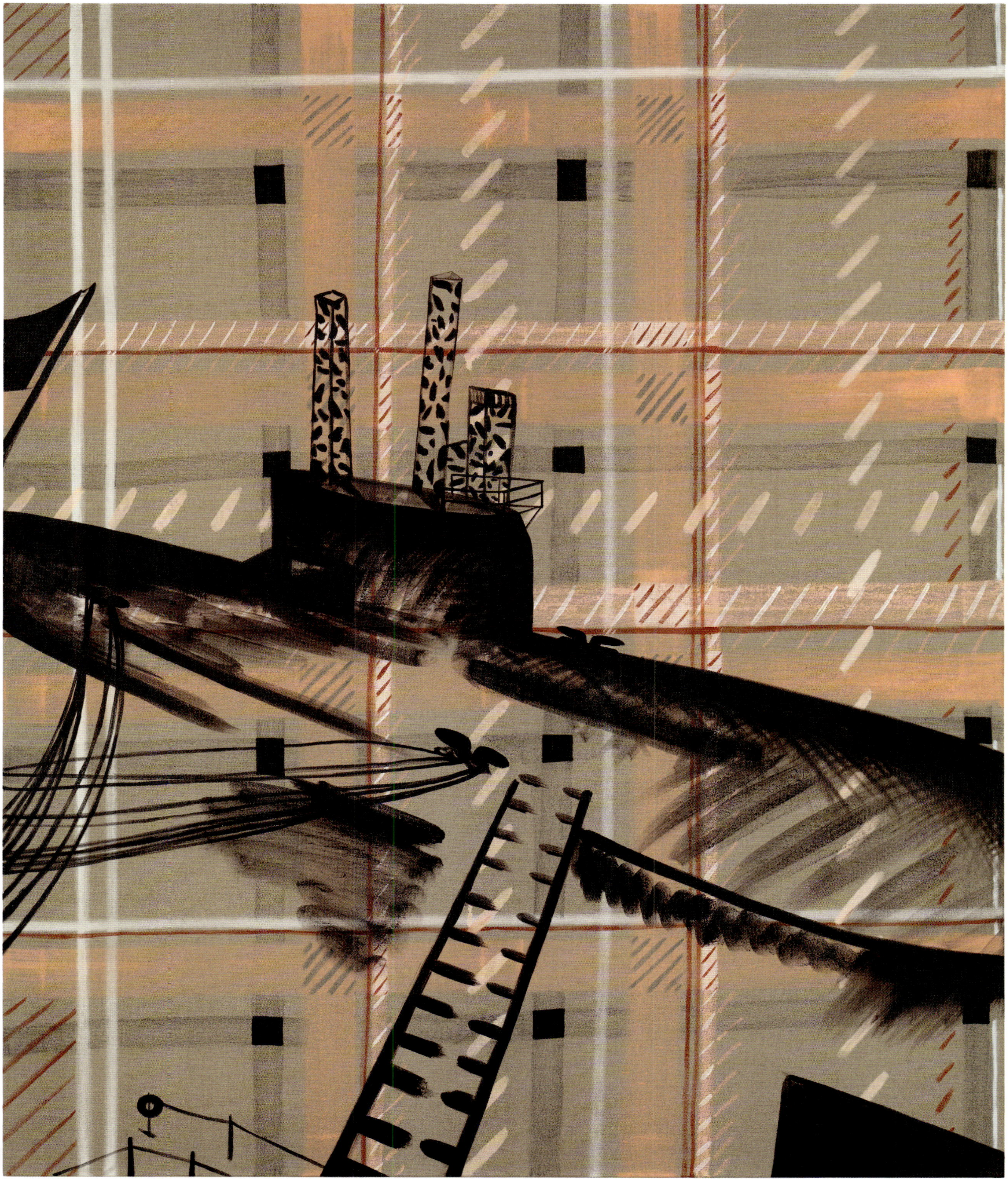

58. Caragh Thuring, *Down Bubble*, 2017

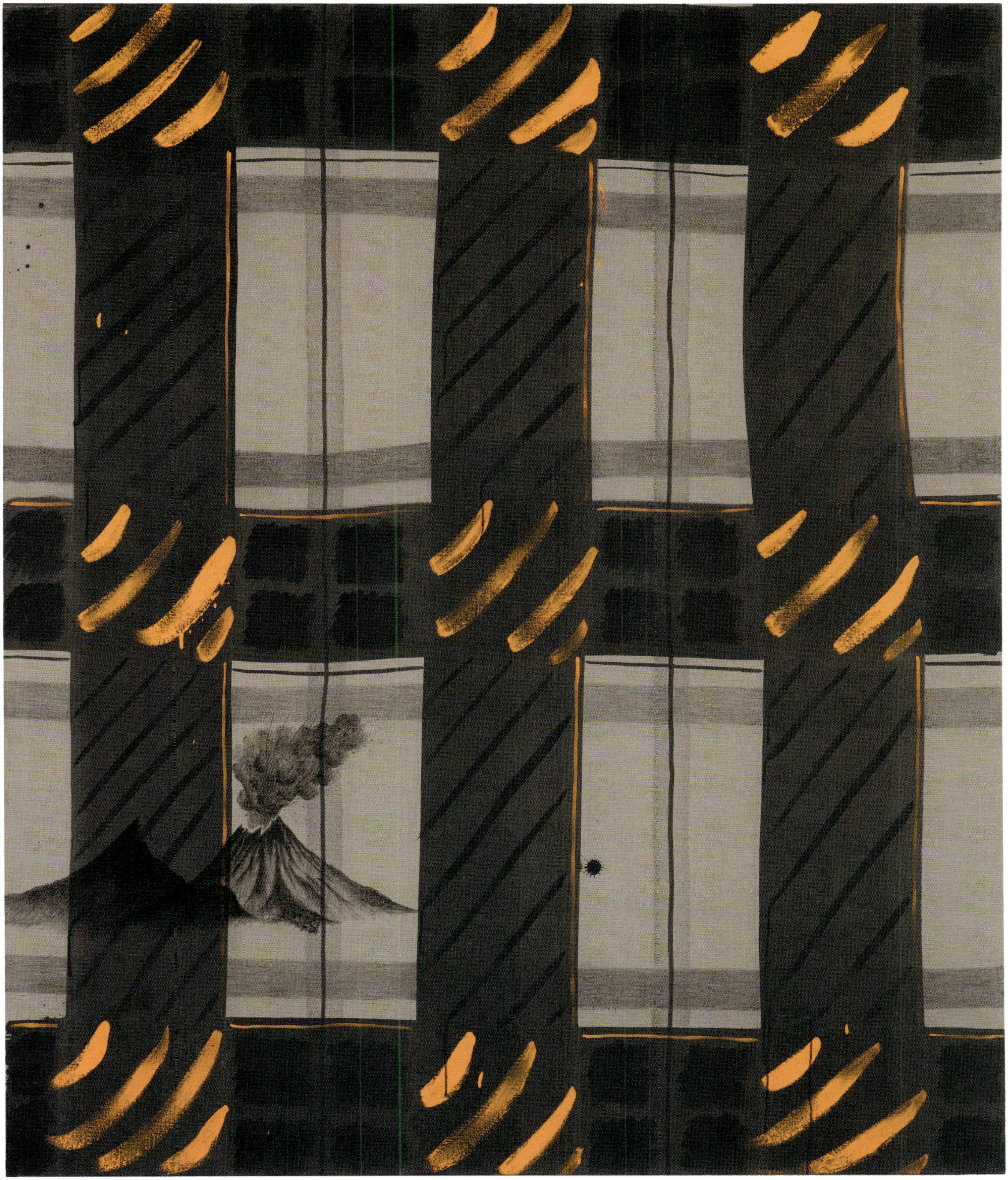

59. Caragh Thuring, *Double Kiss*, 2018

ROUNDTABLE WITH HETTIE JUDAH, GARETH CADWALLADER, ALLISON KATZ AND SHERMAN MERN TAT SAM

HETTIE JUDAH Let's start with the idea of 'slow painting'. I've written about art that's not necessarily slow in terms of the making process but slow because it demands the viewer to spend time in thoughtful engagement with the work. That seems important now, particularly as a resistance to the accelerated looking encouraged by the digital realm. Do you have any feelings about the term? Do you find it a useful way to talk about painting?

GARETH CADWALLADER Do you think there's a correlation between how slowly the thing comes about and how slowly the viewer has to engage with it?

ALLISON KATZ Not necessarily, no. To me the term 'slow painting' is a subjective concept. From the viewer's perspective, so much depends on context: where you're encountering the work, what state you're in for contemplation and how it might correlate to what you're already looking at, thinking about or reading, for instance. As for the artist, I think it's interesting how paintings can conceal their labour. One of painting's qualities that I appreciate is that you can't necessarily tell the time it took to make: a gesture could have taken a long time but looks like it happened really quickly, and vice versa.

GC [John Singer] Sargent's paintings look like they're done really fast but apparently he was very methodical with each brushstroke: actually they're really time-consuming and considered.

SHERMAN MERN TAT SAM Also the time between each brushstroke can be long.

HJ Yes, with Frank Auerbach, you get him scraping the paint off every day and actually the final painting happens in a day but it's taken maybe three months to get to that point.

AK I think that's always been painting's procedural grip. You don't necessarily know how it was made, or why, or how long it took. I find that the term 'slow painting' privileges the slow over the fast as a value, but to me, that seems something painting deliberately sets out to complicate. Not many visual languages contain that ambiguity, both in how the works get made and in their potential digestion. Advertising is clearly a fast medium, and a three-hour film is slow.

SMTS Well, it depends on what happens in the three hours. *Avengers: Endgame* [2019] is three hours long but it's very, very fast.

AK Right, but it has a set time. Painting is free from duration: there's no fixed duration on a painting.

SMTS The joy of painting is that you can see it fast and slow: the freedom is yours. For a three-hour film you have to be there three hours to see it. I like the idea of slow painting. Actually I am a slow painter because physically it takes time. We live in a world of fast looking, so by definition slow looking seems like a nice idea. What is fast painting? [Critic] Rob Colvin uses the term 'like art' referring to painting that looks like other painting: you instantly 'know' what you're looking at because in your mind it's actually something else. Maybe that's fast painting? To me very good painting is slow painting because it takes time to look at.

GC [American painter] Morris Louis said he thought the best time span to look at one of his pictures was about five seconds and then you should move on.

HJ How do you start thinking about a painting? Sherman, can we talk about your drawings?

SMTS My drawings are made in parallel with the paintings: I see them as the same. I started to draw because, when I moved to London, I didn't have a studio for two years. The friends I was staying with said, 'You can't not be an artist, so just draw.' I travel a lot so when I travel I draw. But it's not like I make the drawing to prepare for the painting. Sometimes what happens in the painting then goes to the drawing, and sometimes the other way round: it can be years before one series of actions happens in the other place.

HJ Does your drawing relate to your experience when you're travelling, or do you just happen to be travelling and drawing at the same time?

SMTS Travelling and drawing. Mostly when I make work, I'm either listening to the radio or watching TV to disengage the mind. There are no references: there is no concept. Maybe there isn't a strategy. I make it up as I go along.

HJ Do you need to get yourself into a certain mental state?

SMTS Usually I work right at the end of the day. I spend a lot of the time looking at the work and then maybe the actions happen very quickly but I've spent the day thinking about them. Some of the works do sit around for years. They have to disappear, be abandoned and then you come back.

HJ Gareth, do you have pictorial material that you draw on? Do you accumulate photographs and postcards?

GC Yes, I think most painters do that. Ideas can come from anywhere: films and TV, conversations, walking down the street. You might do a doodle or sketch and that will rest in your head for years. Gradually, by working on it, things get added and taken away until it's quite different. Freud writes [in *The Interpretation of Dreams*, 1899] about how you experience things that seem 'psychologically significant'. They end up in your dreams and are either used for what they are – if they are significant – or you can use something more trivial to say the same thing. That's how my work comes together. It's from all over the place: a lot of the time it's so complicated that you would never be able to trace where it all came from. You just end up with something that seems to click.

HJ Allison, do you use found imagery? Do you take photographs?

AK Yes, I use found imagery – but all imagery is found. I also take photographs, if necessary, but not in a programmatic way. I make no distinction. I make thumbnail sketches for paintings, nothing more, otherwise I lose energy for the real thing. In general I don't like to think too much about composition or formal concerns. The primary energy for painting comes from its relation to life: a kind of coded rephrasing of experience, of reactions to people, events, objects. I see representation as managing the way in which imagery is both claimed and emptied out, how it can be equally felt and performed.

HJ When you're in this preparatory stage, is it as much to do with creating a kind of psychological state for the painting?

AK That stage is constant throughout the process, it changes, and it's never guaranteed. I guess it's always a struggle with meaning, with feeling. I don't want a narrative. I have to recognise something personal in an image that's impersonal, and then the painting can occur.

SMTS Personal to you?

AK Personal to me, yes.

SMTS Does it have to be personal to others?

AK That's not my concern. Or rather, how could it not be personal to someone else, since I am not prescribing a fixed meaning? Everyone understands the world from their own perspective, and at the same time, we overlap and share meaning. At other times we don't, and this is the chance for an artwork to add to, or change, our worldview. To take an image of a rooster – which has the capacity to be both an empty sign and a loaded metaphor – and to charge it with something that's coded for some way of thinking about the world or interpersonal relations – that is my work, and then the viewer activates their own cosmos or chain of associations when looking at it.

HJ Do you approach getting into a painting knowing quite precisely what you're intending to create or is it more free-form?

AK I always just want to know 50 per cent and then something happens. In that sense it feels marked by time, spontaneous, uncertain, like a conversation.

GC I'm quite near knowing precisely what I want to do in terms of what the painting is going to look like, but then you don't really know what you've made. You know it's a picture of X, Y and Z but you don't really know what that is, why you've done that or what that's going to do inside other people's heads.

SMTS I don't ever know what I'm doing. I don't actually have an image. I make the panels first and the panels are all different shapes, so that's the closest to a beginning point or knowing what I'm doing, but I really don't have an idea that it'll end the way it does.

HJ How does one painting relate to another? Do you work in series?

AK I don't actively intend to make a series. I just get hooked. Over time there's been a self-organising persistence of a motif. I start something and think of it as a subject happening once: if it feels like it's exponentially gaining force then I'll return to it. This has been going on with certain motifs for years. It's never intentional and it's happening so slowly that I've never shown those paintings together yet, and anyhow that isn't the point – they are not all made at once with the intention of building a 'body of work' and then moving on. It's a more cyclical, web-like map.

HJ Does one work seem to come out of the one before it? Do you see a relationship, or are they very separate entities?

GC I like the idea of working in a series. I haven't done one, but if I did I'd like it to be super strategic, where the whole thing is like writing a novel, where each work relates very specifically to all the other ones and you wouldn't get one without the others: they would make less sense individually. Just raising the level of ambition.

HJ Gareth, in your last exhibition [*Half-Lowered Eyelids*, 2019, at Josh Lilley, London] there was a clear body of concerns. There's a mood, there are motifs that repeat: how would you describe the relationship between a body of work like that, if series isn't a useful term?

GC Series implies that you're doing it deliberately, whereas with those paintings it was more the same things over and over again. I started painting people looking at fruit, for example, because if you have the subject matter then you can concentrate on everything else. If you have some restrictions, you can gain more freedom in other areas. I was trying to develop a painting style: if you don't have to think about subject matter you can get on with that. When that becomes a bit boring you can look into subject matter again. You start breaking the rules that you set for yourself and that can lead to other ideas.

HJ Where did the idea of people looking at fruit come from?

GC It was on [the packaging of] a salad in a French supermarket: this guy looking at a tomato. A respectable middle-aged man with silver-fox hair and a nice shirt, so absorbed looking at the tomato that he's disappearing. His face is out of focus but his hand and the tomato are in focus. You don't see something like that and understand immediately why you like it but the idea of focusing and being absorbed in something seemed very attractive. Also, that sort of focus reminded me of what it feels like when the painting is going really well. If you're in the studio and you get into the painty world, that's a nice place to be.

HJ Do you work on a body of paintings in parallel with one another or does one lead on from the next one? How do they relate?

GC Sometimes I'll try to work on more than one at a time but basically I can't. I just have to get into that painting for as long as it takes, then by the time I've done that maybe I'll have an idea of what the next thing is. The preparatory stuff goes on in the background as a separate practice, but for the actual painting it seemed really important to focus on one thing at a time.

SMTS So, you're the guy with the tomato?

GC Yes!

AK I work on five, six, seven paintings all at once and each one is very different. That's partly to avoid autopilot – with my own handwriting, with questions of style, with the origin of an image. It's everything to avoid an unquestioned belief.

GC What do you mean by that?

AK I think painting balances belief and doubt. I don't want to get too sure about what I am working on as it is happening – in order to work on it with total commitment. But from a practical point of view, painting is so habit-based that I feel it's part of the challenge to undo the idea of practice. In my mind it's a problem that you can get lost in habits (negative and positive) so easily and lose sight of what could be more interesting about a painting.

GC I made a drunken memo a few weeks ago saying, 'Do things you haven't done before'. I've never done a painting with borders: do a painting with borders because you haven't done it before. Don't fall into habits or otherwise you'll end up losing interest.

AK Or more importantly, the painting won't be interesting. It's not about you. It's all about remembering how to get out of your own way. There's got to be a certain amount of detachment because the process can take a while, so that initial flurry of excitement can get atomised or distributed in different ways. A certain level of unpredictability seems really crucial. Also to never have the surface become too much of an illusion or facade.

HJ You use sand sometimes, don't you?

AK Yes, and rice. I like the realism of these textures since they cannot become illusion. If you can see the sand, it doesn't matter what the paint is doing: the surface will always interrupt or contradict the image.

HJ Sherman, you work on paintings in parallel for years: how many do you have on the go, and for how long?

SMTS It's only 38 (I know because I counted recently). The span of time is more than ten years now, if not longer, because I've been in that studio for 20 years. The fastest painting I've painted is nine months, I think. The longest painting – I lose track after about three years – but I think is about seven to ten.

AK How do they relate to one another?

SMTS They are groupings rather than series. Sometimes they're groupings after the fact. Most summers I make the panels but sometimes they don't get used for a few years. The shape is then decided by what happened the previous year. They have evolved into slightly taller shapes, narrower than the golden section [proportion]. When I start, there are maybe three or four ready, so a group of them has splatters and then another group has zigzag lines that stop the painting. Another has what a friend of mine calls 'angry corners' because they were all red painted corners. As the paintings evolve maybe all these things disappear and they migrate from one group to another.

HJ How tactically do you use colour?

SMTS Before I moved into my studio the palettes were very individual, they were all over the place, so I decided I was only going to paint with five colours. Over time the palette has migrated. I don't mix my colours – they just come out of the tube – so the selection happens in the paint shop. One of the jokes I have with my friends is that I don't paint with blue or purple, and I won't tell them it's just because I was too cheap to buy purple paint. A friend gave me some blue paint, so blue appeared in the palette.

HJ Gareth, with your citrus fruit you immediately get these pops of yellow and orange coming, which are very strong. Can you tell me about the way the colours are working?

GC You're essentially trying to do this world-building thing, so if the colour seems to suit the mood of the world that you want to build, then it will naturally end up being that choice. I do a thumbnail sketch to figure out colour compositions. What if he were wearing a red shirt? Or a yellow shirt? How would that change things? Then you play around until you see something that works. In *Pile of Oranges* [2017] I was careful to make sure the oranges were the only warm colour: everything else is blue or green, basically. That way you can make sure they're spiky enough. You can use them as a patch of colour just to make it visually interesting.

HJ Allison, does this come into your resistance to autopilot? Do you challenge yourself like that?

AK Yes, I think there's a lot of hidden meaning in colour. I love this thing Virginia Woolf said – that she liked to be very mixed. There is so much being communicated already simply by the depth to which a colour has been mixed, and then in how it can be placed in relation to colours straight from the tube. Saturation, opacity, transparency: the way colour is employed is parallel to psychological states as well.

GC In Vermeer's painting *Woman Reading a Letter* [1663–64], her face is the same colour as the map in the background: you can use colour in that way to draw unexpected connections. It's something you see in how Kerry James Marshall uses colour. He talks about invisibility in relation to his work: I like the idea that you can either give something a massive contrast or you can really hide something so the viewer might have to discover it for themselves.

HJ What else have you been looking at recently, and how does it relate to what you're doing?

GC My relationship to historical painting is the same as my relationship to anything – a table, a sofa. If I can take something from it then I will.

HJ Sherman?

SMTS Most of what I like is twentieth-century painting but I do like pre-twentieth-century [art too]. In a way I feel the same way: it's a resource, it's like a library. You look at art and it gives to you when you don't expect it. My paintings are objects, they live in the world and they relate to other things in the world but also to art. When you paint, you automatically relate to the history of painting, consciously or unconsciously. Now there might be artists who come from a more conceptual background and make paintings, but I think their work will eventually be subsumed into its relationship to other paintings. It's very, very hard to stay pure.

GC Unless you're a five-year-old.

SMTS They are the best.

HJ Allison, how does your painting relate to your work in other media?

AK I make graphic posters because there are urges I want to satisfy, to make certain things that painting cannot do. I stopped trying to make painting do everything. I think what Sherman was saying about how everything is absorbed into a painting discourse is really crucial. Every brush mark can be considered a quote. That is part of the pleasure and part of the difficulty. I cannot help but think about the context of painting. I'm looking now in particular at a Goya portrait, *The Black Duchess* [1797]. He signed his name in the sand and the Duchess of Alba is pointing to it. After restoration it was revealed he actually painted *solo Goya* ('only Goya'), a way for him to imagine that his desire towards her was mutual. It's a completely bold gesture: very public and at the same time very private. Capturing the impermanent gesture of writing in the sand with the permanent gesture of oil painting is for me very moving. It's such an economy of means to try to overcome materiality.

HJ What else do you look at? Children's art? Folk art? Graffiti?

GC I actually based a painting [*Egg*, 2018, pl. 13] on something a child had done. Sometimes I teach children at the RA [Royal Academy of Arts] and this kid made a cardboard sculpture of a woman holding an egg on a table, and there's a big light bulb above her head. The light bulb is because she's having an idea and the idea is to stop the egg from rolling off the table. Her mum and I were saying: 'Why should she stop the egg running off the table?' 'Because eggs are messy and you don't want them to fall on the floor.' It seemed like an interesting idea: eggs are a big Freudian thing as well. Heavily loaded subject matter can come from anywhere, can't it?

HJ Sherman, do you look at children's art or marks? Are there things that you find particularly exciting?

SMTS Children's toys, but more broadly design. I like all plastic children's toys, mainly because they come up with awkward shapes. Comic books, but less so now: I like the older hand-drawn stuff. If you look at pre-1970s comics, when they were really unregulated, the narratives were not super good. You see a lot of strange things.

HJ I feel this exhibition is conceived as a counterpoint to the attention economy of our digital culture. How do you relate to the technological and digital realms?

GC I'd like to try to make paintings that you cannot see on a computer screen, because then you reactivate the point of paintings existing in real life. There was a trend a few years ago: galleries started closing but still had an online or art fair presence. I'd like to make anti-art-fair painting, where you have to be in a quiet place and give it proper attention: one-on-one engagement.

AK I use Photoshop to construct my paintings all the time, but they don't look like Photoshop. It's just about transitions. I can make an intimate mark with pen on paper, put it through Photoshop, project it, and then slowly paint a massively enlarged version with a brush. So it looks spontaneous, but it's not. In that sense, technology can actually slow you down. I don't think it's just painting's dilemma to be seen on a screen, it's all aspects of life. It's fashion. It's humans. You see them in person and you think, 'Wow. You don't look like your photo.'

HJ Winding up, I want to come back to the idea of slow painting. There has been some discussion here about ways of seeing, art on screens, and leaving things for people to work out for themselves. Allison's talked about resisting autopilot, and not falling into belief. All this seems to express a desire not to go for the easy route. Is that a useful way of talking about slow painting?

AK I think it's a way of talking about painting.

HJ I think people look at paintings and are aware there was a body involved in making them: they feel a particular attraction to them.

AK Yes, because paintings have a different temporal presence, different energy.

SMTS It's a primal connection, I think, which is why spiritual and 'outsider' art is popular. I think the business of the contemporary art world – including the biennials – has marginalised the emotive. If you look at what's being shown, there are very few emotive works, in terms of their physical presence. Everything is very manufactured.

GC Maybe it's taste: the things that I end up attracted to do provide a slower pace. I think that for me, slowness is connected to 'world-building' – the necessarily slow process of taking elements from reality and reconfiguring them in a painting. Something I still struggle with, though, is locating the point at which that world-building becomes a meaningful way of engaging with reality as opposed to just running away from it.

DARREN ALMOND

Born 1971, Wigan, UK. Lives and works in London, UK.

1 *Somewhere Between I*, 2018
Aquacryl on aluminium
50 × 40 × 3
Courtesy the artist and White Cube

2 *Somewhere Between VII*, 2018
Aquacryl on aluminium
50 × 40 × 3
Courtesy the artist and White Cube

3 *Somewhere Between XVI*, 2018
Aquacryl on aluminium
60 × 50 × 3
Courtesy the artist and White Cube

4 *Somewhere Between XVIII*, 2018
Aquacryl on aluminium
50 × 40 × 3
Courtesy the artist and White Cube

ATHANASIOS ARGIANAS

Born 1976, Athens, Greece. Lives and works in London, UK, and Athens, Greece.

5 *reading paintings (no1, binaural microphone & post-it notes)*, 2019
Acrylic and gouache on card, artist frame
Two parts, each 35 × 40, unframed
Courtesy the artist

6 *reading paintings (no2, binaural microphone & post-it notes)*, 2019
Acrylic and gouache on board, artist frame
Two parts, each 35 × 40, unframed
Courtesy the artist

MICHAEL ARMITAGE

Born 1984, Nairobi, Kenya. Lives and works in London, UK.

9 *Balcony*, 2013
Oil on lubugo bark cloth
210 × 160
Private Collection, London

7 *Kariakor*, 2015
Oil on lubugo bark cloth
170 × 150
Arts Council Collection, Southbank Centre, London

8 *Mpeketoni*, 2015
Oil on lubugo bark cloth
195.6 × 149.9
The Pisces Collection

GARETH CADWALLADER

Born 1979, Swindon, UK. Lives and works in London, UK.

10 *Bath*, 2015–16
Oil on canvas
28 × 22
Private collection. Courtesy Corvi-Mora, London

11 *Bed*, 2017
Oil on canvas
27.8 × 20.2
Courtesy private collection

12 *Milk*, 2017
Oil on canvas
27 × 22
Collection of Josh Lilley, London

13 *Egg*, 2018
Oil on canvas
27 × 22
Private collection, London

VARDA CAIVANO

Born 1971, Buenos Aires, Argentina. Lives and works in London, UK.

14 *Untitled*, 2011
Oil on canvas
50.8 × 76.2
Arts Council Collection, Southbank Centre, London

16 *Untitled*, 2012–18
Oil on canvas
110 × 86
Courtesy the artist and Victoria Miro, London/Venice

17 *Untitled*, 2018
Oil on canvas
50 × 40
Courtesy the artist and Victoria Miro, London/Venice

15 *Untitled*, 2018
Oil on canvas
100 × 70
Courtesy the artist and Victoria Miro, London/Venice

LUBAINA HIMID

Born 1954, Zanzibar. Lives and works in Preston, UK.

18 *Garfoni*, 1995
Acrylic on canvas
153 × 122
Courtesy the artist and Hollybush Gardens, London

19 *Le Rodeur: The Exchange*, 2016
Acrylic on canvas
183 × 244
Courtesy the artist and Hollybush Gardens, London

PAUL HOUSLEY

Born 1964, Stalybridge, Greater Manchester, UK. Lives and works in London, UK.

20 *Grey Monarch*, 2019
Oil on canvas
70 × 50
Courtesy the artist and Belmacz

21 *Prizes for Creeps*, 2019
Oil on found object (board and frame)
94 × 72, including frame
Courtesy the artist and Belmacz

22 *Slow Dance in the Long Game*, 2019
Oil on canvas
40 × 30
Courtesy the artist and Belmacz

23 *Two Painters*, 2019
Oil on canvas
120 × 100
Courtesy the artist and Belmacz

Plates are organised in chronological order. All dimensions are given in centimetres, and are height × width × depth.

MERLIN JAMES
Born 1960, Cardiff, Wales. Lives and works in Glasgow, Scotland.

27 *Bay*, 1998
Acrylic and mixed media on canvas
56 × 71
Courtesy Sikkema Jenkins & Co., New York

24 *Chien*, 2006–10
Acrylic on canvas
51 × 38
Courtesy Sikkema Jenkins & Co., New York

25 *Hanger*, 2016
Mixed media (wood, acrylic, fabric)
69 × 109
Courtesy Kerlin Gallery, Dublin

26 *Mirror*, 2019
Acrylic on canvas
36 × 52.5
Courtesy Kerlin Gallery, Dublin

ALLISON KATZ
Born 1980, Montreal, Canada. Lives and works in London, UK.

31 *Double Hunger*, 2015
Oil on canvas
195 × 179
Private collection, Milan, and Gio Marconi, Milan. Courtesy the artist

29 *AKgraph (All Is On)*, 2016
Acrylic on canvas
200 × 130
Courtesy Alexander V. Petalas

30 *Elf-Esteem*, 2017
Oil and acrylic on linen
130 × 95
Courtesy the artist and The Approach, London

28 *Snowglobe*, 2018
Acrylic and sand on canvas
175 × 125
Courtesy Daskal Collection

SIMON LING
Born 1968, Keighley, UK. Lives and works in London, UK.

32 *Untitled*, 2016
Oil on canvas
183 × 122
Courtesy the artist and greengrassi, London

33 *Untitled*, 2018
Acrylic on paper
Overall, 304 × 287.5
15 parts, each 76 × 57.5
Courtesy the artist and greengrassi, London

LUCY MCKENZIE
Born 1977, Glasgow, Scotland. Lives and works in Brussels, Belgium.

34 *Quodlibet XI (Janette Murray)*, 2011
Oil on canvas
80 × 55 × 2.5
Collection Nicoletta Fiorucci Russo, London

35 *Quodlibet XXXIV*, 2014
Oil on canvas
180 × 130
Courtesy Defares Collection

MAIREAD O'HEOCHA
Born 1962, Dublin, Ireland, where she lives and works.

38 *Flowers and Herakles*, 2015
Oil on board
86 × 63
Courtesy private collection, Dublin

36 *Cabinet of Herons, Natural History Museum*, 2018
Oil on board
84 × 63
Courtesy the artist and mother's tankstation, Dublin/London

37 *Still Life with Skull, Coral and Flowers*, 2018
Oil on board
72 × 84
Courtesy private collection, Dublin

YELENA POPOVA
Born in 1978, Urals, Russia. Lives and works in Nottingham, UK.

39 *Low Parkamoor, 200 Metres above the East Shore of Lake Coniston, Cumbria*, 2018–19
From *Post Petrochemical* series, 2017–ongoing
Soil and wood ash distemper on canvas
153 × 117
Courtesy the artist

40 *2.5Gs (2.5 Gigaseconds)*, 2019
From *Evaporating Paintings* series, 2015–ongoing
Prussian blue, zinc white, pale cerulean, distemper on linen
153 × 117
Courtesy the artist

CAROL RHODES
Born 1959, Edinburgh, Scotland. Died 2018, Glasgow, Scotland.

41 *Buildings*, 1994
Oil on board
47 × 39.5
Paintings in Hospitals Collection

44 *Caravans, View*, 1995–97
Oil on board
46 × 45.5
Paintings in Hospitals Collection

43 *Industrial Landscape*, 1997
Oil on board
42.5 × 47.5
Arts Council Collection, Southbank Centre, London

42 *Factory Roof, Countryside*, 2002
Oil on board
47 × 57
Southampton City Art Gallery

SHERMAN MERN TAT SAM
Born 1966, Singapore. Lives and works in London, UK, and Singapore.

48 *Whole Lotta Love*, 2012
Oil on panel
35.7 × 27.2
Courtesy the artist

46 *Common Ground*, 2014
Oil on panel
38.6 × 33.9
Courtesy Lymyfyr Art Consultancy

47 *Just a Perfect Day*, 2014
Oil on panel
54.4 × 40.1
Courtesy the artist

45 *Disco Heaven*, 2015
Oil on panel
41.6 × 34.4
Courtesy the artist

BENJAMIN SENIOR
Born 1982, Southampton, UK.
Lives and works in London, UK.

52 *Portals*, 2016
Oil on linen
100 × 80
Courtesy Hubert Zandberg, London, UK

51 *Summersend*, 2018
Egg tempera on cotton on plywood
60 × 50
Courtesy Hubert Zandberg, London, UK

49 *Old Town*, 2019
Egg tempera on cotton on plywood
50 × 60
Courtesy the artist and Carl Freedman Gallery

50 *Shade*, 2019
Egg tempera on cotton on plywood
40 × 50
Courtesy the artist and Carl Freedman Gallery

MICHAEL SIMPSON
Born 1940, Dorset, UK.
Lives and works in Wiltshire, UK.

53 *Squint 59*, 2017
Oil on canvas
230 × 214
Courtesy the artist and Blain|Southern

TIM STONER
Born 1970, Essex, UK. Lives and works in London, UK, and Ronda, Spain.

54 *Día de los muertos (Casares)*, 2016–19
Oil on linen
204 × 245
Courtesy Stuart Shave/Modern Art, London

56 *Jardín (Ronda)*, 2018
Oil on canvas
50 × 50
Courtesy Stuart Shave/Modern Art, London

55 *Virgen de la Cabeza (Ronda)*, 2019
Oil and charcoal on linen
55 × 73.5
Courtesy Stuart Shave/Modern Art, London

CARAGH THURING
Born 1972, Brussels, Belgium.
Lives and works in London, UK, and Argyll, Scotland.

58 *Down Bubble*, 2017
Oil, graphite on linen
165.1 × 137.2
Private collection, London

59 *Double Kiss*, 2018
Graphite, pigment, oil, charcoal on linen
165.1 × 137.16
Thomas Dane, London

57 *Roger*, 2018
Oil, oil stick, gesso, pigment, acrylic on dyed linen
213.4 × 152.4
Courtesy the artist and Thomas Dane Gallery, London

Martin Herbert is a writer and art critic. He is Associate Editor of *ArtReview* and a regular contributor to *Artforum*, *frieze* and *Art Monthly*. Herbert's books include *Mark Wallinger* (2011), *The Uncertainty Principle* (2014), *Tell Them I Said No* (2016) and *Unfold This Moment* (2019).

Hettie Judah is a writer and art critic. Her writing has been published in *frieze*, the *Guardian*, the *i*, and the *New York Times*, among others. She is the author of *Art London* (2019), and a forthcoming biography of Frida Kahlo.

The publisher has made every effort to contact all copyright holders. If proper acknowledgement has not been made, we ask copyright holders to contact the publisher. All works are © the artist unless otherwise stated:

© Charline von Heyl 2019 p. 8;
© Benjamin Senior, 2019 p. 9, plates 49–52;
© Michael Simpson, 2019 p. 11, plate 53;
© Lubaina Himid, 2019 p. 12, plates 18–19;
© Merlin James, 2019 p. 13 (bottom), plates 24–27;
© Njideka Akunyili Crosby p. 14;
© Michael Armitage plates 7–9;
© Varda Caivano plates 14–17;
© Paul Housley plates 20–23;
© Yelena Popova, 2019 plates 39–40;
© Tim Stoner plates 54–56;
© Caragh Thuring plates 57–59.

All images are courtesy the artist unless otherwise stated:

Courtesy Galerie Buchholz, Berlin/Cologne/New York p. 7; courtesy the artist and Petzel, New York p. 8; courtesy the artist and BolteLang, Zurich p. 9; courtesy the artist and Blain|Southern (photo: Peter Mallet) p. 11; Government Art Collection. Courtesy the artist and Hollybush Gardens (photo: Andy Keate) p. 12; courtesy Ceysson and Bénétière p. 13 (top); courtesy the artist and Kerlin Gallery, Dublin p. 13 (bottom); courtesy the artist, Victoria Miro and David Zwirner p. 14.

Courtesy White Cube and the artist plates 1–4; courtesy the artist (photo: Anna Arca) plates 5–6; photo © White Cube (George Darrell) plate 7; photo © White Cube (Prudence Cuming Associates Ltd) plates 8–9; courtesy the artist and Corvi-Mora, London plate 10 (photo: Marcus Leith); courtesy the artist and Victoria Miro, London/Venice plates 15–17; Arts Council Collection, Southbank Centre, London plate 14; courtesy the artist and Hollybush Gardens (photo: Andy Keate) plates 18–19; courtesy the artist and Belmacz (photo: FXP Photography) plates 20–23; courtesy the artist and Sikkema Jenkins & Co., New York plates 24–25; courtesy the artist and Kerlin Gallery, Dublin plates 26–27; courtesy the artist, private collection, Dubai and The Approach, London (photo: © Plastiques Photography 2018) plate 28; courtesy the artist, Collection of Alexander V. Petalas, The Approach, London (photo: © FXP Photography 2016) plate 29; courtesy the artist and The Approach, London plate 30; courtesy the artist, private collection, Milan, and Gio Marconi, Milan and The Approach, London (photo: Filippo Armellin, 2016) plate 31; courtesy greengrassi, London (photo: Marcus Leith) plates 32–33; courtesy the artist and Cabinet, London plates 34–35; courtesy the artist and mother's tankstation Dublin | London plates 36–38; courtesy the Estate of the artist and Merlin James plates 41–42, 44; Arts Council Collection, Southbank Centre, London plate 43; courtesy Carl Freedman Gallery (photo: Peter Mallet) plates 49–50; courtesy Carl Freedman Gallery (photo: Andy Keate) plates 51–52; courtesy the artist and Blain|Southern (photo: Trevor Good) plate 53; courtesy Stuart Shave/Modern Art, London (photo: Robert Glowacki) plates 54–56; courtesy the artist and Thomas Dane Gallery (photo: Richard Ivey) plates 57–58; courtesy the artist and Thomas Dane Gallery (photo: Ben Westoby) plate 59.

Slow Painting was conceived by Martin Herbert, and developed and organised by Hayward Gallery Touring.

We are deeply indebted to the exhibiting artists, who have all responded generously to our invitation to participate.

The following individuals and institutions have kindly lent to the exhibition, together with those who wish to remain anonymous:

Arts Council Collection
Daskal Collection
Defares Collection
Collection Nicoletta Fiorucci Russo
Josh Lilley
Lymyfyr Art Consultancy
Paintings in Hospitals
Southampton Art Gallery
Hubert Zandberg
The Pisces Collection

Hayward Gallery Touring would like to express our utmost thanks to our partners in the four cities that this exhibition will tour, whose commitment has made *Slow Painting* possible:

Sarah Brown, Principal Keeper, Leeds Art Gallery
Priscila Buschinelli, Programme and Exhibitions Manager, The Edge, University of Bath
Dr Sarah Chapman, Artistic Director, The Arts Institute, University of Plymouth
Mary Costello, Exhibitions Coordinator, The Arts Institute, University of Plymouth
Jamie Eastman, Director of Arts, University of Bath
Cathy Shankland, Exhibitions Officer, Inverness Museum & Art Gallery
Elizabeth Simpson, Curator of Exhibitions, Leeds Art Gallery
Professor Anita Taylor, Executive Dean, Bath School of Art & Design, Bath Spa University
Lucy Woodley, Exhibitions Craft & Design, Inverness Museum & Art Gallery

Finally, we are immensely grateful for all the help received in organising the exhibition, and would like to thank the following individuals and institutional staff members for their invaluable guidance and assistance in securing the works for the tour:

Matilda Agace, Archive & Liaison, Belmacz
Ned Armstrong, Studio Varda Caivano
Irene Bradbury, Director of Artist Liaison, White Cube
Freddie Checketts, Gallery Manager, Cabinet Gallery
Bridget Chew, Studio Manager, Darren Almond
Tommaso Corvi-Mora, Director, Corvi-Mora Gallery
Robert Diament, Director, Carl Freedman Gallery
Tom Dingle, Director, Thomas Dane Gallery
Jess Fletcher, Associate Director & Artist Liaison, Blain | Southern
Carl Freedman, Director, Carl Freedman Gallery
Cornelia Grassi, Director, greengrassi
Hannah Gruy, Artist and Museum Liaison, White Cube
Jo Harrison, Assistant Director, The Approach
Finola Jones, Director, mother's tankstation
Amisha Karia, Head of Collection, Paintings in Hospitals
Marina La Verghetta, Assistant Curator, Fiorucci Art Trust
Rachel Lepley, Executive Assistant to Alexander V. Petalas
Martin McGeown, Director, Cabinet Gallery
Kirk McInroy, Director, Stuart Shave/Modern Art
Clare Mitchell, Curator of Art, Southampton Art Gallery
Jake Miller, Partner/Director, The Approach
Andrew Mummery, Director, A-M-G5
Lisa Panting, Co-director Hollybush Gardens
Alice Paton, Registrar, Victoria Miro
William Pym, Director, Josh Lilley Gallery
Olivia Rawnsley, Registrar, Thomas Dane Gallery
Jess Reid, National Loans Coordinator, Paintings in Hospitals
Emma Robertson, Partner/Director, The Approach
Malin Ståhl, Co-director, Hollybush Gardens
Georgia Spickett-Jones, Archivist, Thomas Dane Gallery
Giulia Tiraboschi, Director, Gio Marconi, Milan
Madelon van Schie, Defares Collection
Jessica Whitfield, Exhibitions Officer, Southampton Art Gallery
Isabelle Young, Exhibitions Assistant, Victoria Miro

Hayward Gallery Touring give thanks to the following people for their contribution in bringing this exhibition to fruition:

HAYWARD GALLERY TOURING
Brian Cass, Senior Curator
Gillian Fox, Exhibition Organiser
Alison Maun, Exhibition Bookings and Indemnity Coordinator
James Coney, Senior Technician

HAYWARD GALLERY
Ralph Rugoff, Director
Marcia Ceppo, Operations & Logistics Manager
Aoife Leach, General Manager
Charlotte Pearson, Registrar

HAYWARD GALLERY PUBLISHING
Alice Nightingale, Art Publisher
Diana Adell, Publishing Project Manager
Alex Glen, Sales Manager

SOUTHBANK CENTRE
Elaine Bedell, Chief Executive
Spirit de la Mere, Press Manager, Visual Arts
James Smyllie, Press Officer, Visual Arts
Filipa Mendes, Senior Press Manager
Vicky Cheetham, Director of Producing and Presentation
Naomi Wilkinson, Finance Business Partner (Artistic, Development and Production)

Published on the occasion of the exhibition:
Slow Painting

Leeds Art Gallery
25 October 2019 – 12 January 2020

The Levinsky Gallery,
The Arts Institute, Plymouth
24 January – 29 March 2020

The Edge, University of Bath,
and the Bath School of Art and Design
10 April – 6 June 2020

Inverness Museum and Art Gallery,
and Thurso Gallery
25 July – 3 October 2020

Curator Martin Herbert
Exhibition Organiser Gillian Fox

This exhibition has been made possible by the provision of insurance through the Government Indemnity Scheme. Hayward Gallery would like to thank HM Government for providing Government Indemnity and the Department for Culture, Media and Sport and Arts Council England for arranging the indemnity.

Published in 2019 by
Hayward Gallery Publishing
Southbank Centre
Belvedere Road
London SE1 8XX
United Kingdom
southbankcentre.co.uk

Art Publisher Alice Nightingale
Publishing Project Manager Diana Adell
Sales Manager Alex Glen
Picture Research Rosie Pickles
Catalogue design Studio Mathias Clottu
Printed in Italy *by* Printer Trento

A catalogue record for this book is available from the British Library.

ISBN 978 1 85332 365 2

Distributed in North America, Central America and South America by
ARTBOOK | D.A.P.
75 Broad Street, Suite 630
New York, NY 10004
+1 212 627 1999
artbook.com

Distributed in the UK and Europe by
Cornerhouse Publications
HOME, 2 Tony Wilson Place
Manchester, M15 4FN
+44 (0)161 212 3466
cornerhousepublications.org

Front cover Gareth Cadwallader, *Bath*, 2015–16
Back cover Merlin James, *Hanger*, 2016 (detail)

HAYWARD GALLERY TOURING
SOUTHBANK CENTRE
LOTTERY FUNDED
Supported using public funding by ARTS COUNCIL ENGLAND